EASY POINTS

Class XII

GEOGRAPHY

Brief and precise notes from NCERT text books for CBSE board exam 2026-27

Compiled By:
Shailendra Singh
PGT Geography
PM Shri School Jawahar Navodaya Vidyalaya,
Pichhore, Distt. Gwalior (Madhya Pradesh)
Email: shail.arsh22@gmail.com

4 June, 2026

With the blessings and inspiration of Shri Rammangal Das Ji Maharaj, This book is dedicated to the students appearing in the annual board examination for Geography subject of class 12th conducted by the Central Board of Secondary Education.

This book is an attempt to make NCERT text book simple and easy for answer writting to the students, so they can learn and practice correct and accurate answers and score maximum marks in their board examination.

Index

Book 1 - Fundamentals of Human Geography

Book 2 - India People and Economy

❖ **Map Based Questions**

BOOK 1 - FUNDAMENTALS OF HUMAN GEOGRAPHY

CHAPTER 1 - HUMAN GEOGRAPHY NATURE AND SCOPE

1. Define the concept of Human Geography.

i. "Human geography is the synthetic study of relationship between human societies and earth's surface". Ratzel

ii. "Human geography is the study of the changing relationship between the unresting man and the unstable earth." E.C. Semple

iii. "Conception resulting from a more synthetic knowledge of the physical laws governing our earth and of the relations between the living beings which inhabit it". Paul Vidal de la Blache.

iv. Human geography offers a new conception of the interrelationships between earth and human beings.

2. Mention the any three dualisms in geography which started wide-ranging debates in the discipline of geography.

The three dualism in geography which started wide-ranging debates in the discipline of geography are:

a. Whether geography as a discipline should be a **law making/theorizing (nomothetic) or descriptive (idiographic).**

b. Whether approach of the study should be **regional or systematic**?

c. Whether geographical phenomena be interpreted **theoretically** or through **historic-institutional** approach?

3. State any six examples of metaphors used to describe the physical and human phenomena.

They are:

i. 'Face' of the earth,

ii. 'Eye' of the storm,

iii. 'Mouth' of the river,

iv. 'Snout' (nose) of the glacier,

v. 'Neck' of the isthmus

vi. 'Profile' of the soil.

vii. Regions, villages, towns have been described as 'organisms'.

viii. Networks of road, railways and water ways are described as "arteries of circulation".

4. **Describe important features of the concept of Natualisation of Humans.**

Environmental deterministic approach states that:

a. Environment controls human actions and activities.

b. Humans were directly dependent on naturalenvironment.

c. Humans were not free and they adapted according to the nature.

d. Humans were naturalized they were afraid of natural forces.

e. It states that human history, culture, life style, and stages of development are influenced by the physical environment like climate, soil, relief, etc.

f. It considers human as passive agents, whose attitude, decision making is influenced by physical environment.

g. Example: the life of nomads or tribal people living in mountains or forests.

5. **State the important characteristics of possibilism approach of human geography.**

Possibilistic approach states that:

a. Humans were free to choose. Nature did not control him.

b. The nature provided possibilities for humans to exploit it for their benefits.

c. It considered humans as active agents rather than a passive one.

d. It's the technology, attitude, habits, values of humans which influenced its action not the nature.

e. The nature got humanized.

6. **State the important characteristics of concept of neo-determinism approach of human geography.**

   Griffith Taylor introduced the concept of neo-determinism of **stop and go determinism**. It states that:

   a. Neither is there a situation of absolute necessity (environmental determinism) nor is there a condition of absolute freedom (possibilism).

   b. It states that nature has provided possibilities and scope for development but also put limits on it.

   c. It means that human beings can conquer nature by obeying it. They can continue in their pursuit of development when nature permits.

   d. The neo-determinism conceptually attempts to bring a balance nullifying the 'either' 'or' dichotomy.

7. **The Scope of Human Geography and its Relationship to Other Social Sciences**

   a. The scope of human geography is extremely broad. Human geography attempts to explain the relationships between all elements of human life.

   b. To understand and explain these human elements, human geography is closely linked with allied social science disciplines. Therefore, human geography is highly interdisciplinary in nature.

   c. Just as new subfields develop with the expansion of knowledge, the subfields of human geography are also linked with social sciences such as history, political science, demography, and economics.

8. **Humanistic Geography**

   a. The welfare ideology of human geography is concerned with the social well-being of people.

   b. It includes aspects such as housing, health, and education.

   c. This theory is more relevant to socio-political reality.

9. **Radical Ideology of Geography.**
   a. This ideology is based on Marxist ideology.
   b. It attempts to explain the causes of poverty, bondage, and social inequality.
   c. Contemporary social problems are considered to be linked to capitalism.

10. **Behavioral Geography**
    a. Behavioral ideology places greater emphasis on understanding human behavior, race, religion, etc.
    b. It gives greater importance to the individual rather than society and groups.
    c. According to this ideology, every person has some impact on the environment.

11. **Development of approaches in human geography.**
    a. **Exploration and Description** - In the early colonial era, imperial expansion and commercial interests encouraged exploration and discovery of new areas, making a comprehensive description of the region an important aspect of geographers' descriptions.
    b. **Regional Analysis** - In the post-colonial era, detailed descriptions of all aspects of a region were emphasized, as all regions are parts of the Earth, and complete knowledge of these regions contributes to a complete understanding of the Earth.
    c. **Regional Differentiation** - The period between the two World Wars saw an attempt to understand how and why one region differs from another. This emphasized identifying the uniqueness of a region.
    d. **Spatial Organization** - From the late 1950s to the late 1960s, the use of computers and statistical methods allowed the application of physical laws to the analysis of maps and human phenomena.
    e. **Emergence of schools of thoughts** - Dissatisfaction with the quantitative revolution and the inhumane approach to

geography led to the emergence of three new schools of thought in human geography in the 1970s: humanistic, radical, and behavioral. These schools of thought made human geography more relevant to socio-political reality.

f. **Post-modernism in geography** - Broad generalizations and the use of global theories to explain the human condition began to be questioned. Since the 1990s, emphasis has been placed on the importance of understanding human development and each local context.

12. "The imprint of human activities is everywhere." Explain this statement with suitable examples.

a. With the development of technology, humans move from deprivation to independence.

b. Human activities create cultural landscapes in the development of resorts (rest houses) on highlands, urban expansion, orchards, and pastures.

c. The use of ports and sea routes in coastal regions are clear examples of human influence.

d. The development of faster communication resources and the development of satellites in space leave human influences everywhere.

Objective

1. Who gave the concept of neo-determinism or stop-and-go determinism?

a) Ratzel   b) E. Sample   c) Griffith Taylor   d) Blache

2. Which of the following approach was not developed in the 1970s?

a) humanist   b) radical   c) pragmatist   d) dualism

3. Behavioral geography is associated with which subject of social science?

a) Anthropology   b) Welfare economics
c) Psychology   d) Sociology

4. **"Human geography is the study of the changing relationship between the unstable earth and the unresting man" - Who presented the above definition of human geography?**
   a) Ratzel   b) Paul Vidal-de-la Blache
   c) Fabre   d) E. C. Sample

5. Which of the following statement does not describe Geography?
a) Integrative Discipline
b) Study of inter-relationship between human beings and environment
c) Based on duality
d) Not relevant in modern times due to the development of technology

6. Which of the following is not a source of geographical information?
a) Details of travelers   b) Ancient maps
c) Samples of rocky materials from the moon   d) Ancient epics

7. Which one of the following is the most important factor in the interaction between people and the environment?
a) Human intelligence   b) Technology
c) Experience of people   d) Human brotherhood

8. Which one of the following is not an approach to human geography?
a) Regional Variation   b) Quantitative Revolution
c) Spatial organization   d) Exploration and description

9. Arrange the following approaches in the order of their development-
1. Regional analysis   2. Areal differentiation
3. Spatial organization   4. Exploration and description
a) 1 4 2 3   b) 4 1 2 3   c) 4 1 3 2   d) 3 2 4 1

10. Assertion (A) : Technology indicates the level of cultural development of a society.
    Reason (R) : Technology developed only after man developed a better understanding of natural laws.
a) Both A and R are true and R is the correct explanation of A.
b) Both A and R are true but R is not the correct explanation of A.
c) A is true but R is false.
d) A is false but R is true.

Answers- 1-c, 2-d, 3-c, 4-d, 5-d, 6-c, 7-d, 8-b, 9-b, 10-a

CHAPTER 2 - THE WORLD POPULATION DISTRIBUTION, DENSITY & GROWTH

1. Define the terms-

a) Population density.

b) Population distribution

c) Population growth or population change

Ans. (a) **<u>Population density</u>** refers to the ratio between numbers of people to the size of land in a country. It is usually measured in persons per sq km.

$$\text{Density of Population} = \frac{\text{Population}}{\text{Area}}$$

(b) **Population distribution** refers to the way people are spaced over the earth's surface.

(c) **Population growth** refers to the change in number of people of a territory during a specific period of time. This change may be positive or negative. It is usually expressed in terms of percentage or numbers.

2. Describe the uneven patterns of population distribution in the world.

a) Broadly, 90 per cent of the world population lives in about 10 per cent of its land area.

b) The 10 most populous countries of the world contribute about 60 per cent of the world's population.

c) Out of top most populated 15 countries, 7 are located in Asia.

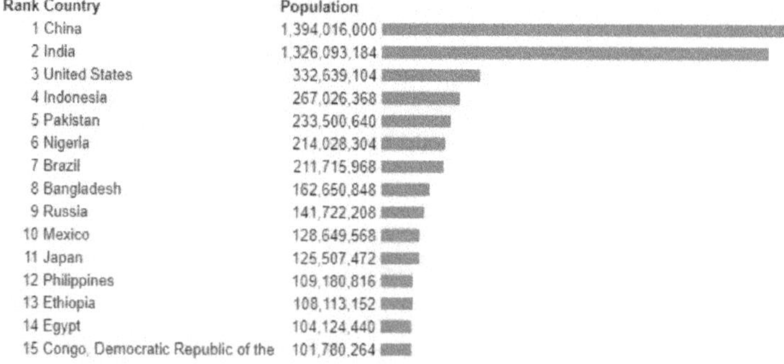

3. Explain, with suitable examples, the factors which influence the population distribution and density in the world.

The factors which influence the population distribution and density in the world are grouped into three categories:

A) <u>Geographical factors</u>:

(i) *Availability of water:* People prefer to live in areas where fresh water is easily available for drinking, industries, crops, cattle and navigation. <u>E.g</u>. It is because of this that **River Valleys** are among the most densely populated areas of the world.

(ii) *Landforms:* People prefer living on flat plains and gentle slopes rather than on mountainous and hilly areas.

   I. This is because plain areas are favourable for the production of crops and to build roads and industries.

   II. Whereas, the mountainous and hilly areas are unfavourable for the development of transport network, agriculture and industries.

   III. <u>E.g</u>. the Ganga plains are among the most densely populated areas of the world while the mountains zones in the Himalayas are barely populated.

(iii) *Climate:*

   I. Areas with a comfortable climate, where there is not much seasonal variation have high population.

   II. Whereas, extreme climates such as very hot or cold, deserts and heavy rainfall are uncomfortable for human living and have low population.

   III. <u>E.g</u>. Mediterranean regions were inhabited from early periods in history due to their pleasant climate.

(iv) *Soils:* Fertile soils are important for agricultural and related activities. Therefore, areas which have fertile loamy soils have more people living on them as these can support intensive agriculture.

B) **<u>Economic Factors</u>**: Minerals, urbanization and industrial development are most important factors which influenced the world population distribution.

i) **Minerals**: Areas with rich mineral deposits attract Mining and industrial activities therefore skilled and semi–skilled workers move to these areas for employment and make them densely populated. *E.g.* Katanga Zambia copper belt in Africa is one such good example.

ii) Urbanisation: le migrate in the cities for better employment opportunities, educational and medical facilities, and better means of transport and communication and good civic amenities. Mega cities of the world continue to attract large number of migrants every year.

iii) **Industrialisation**: Industrial belts provide job opportunities and attract large numbers of people. These include not just factory workers but also transport operators, shopkeepers, bank employees, doctors, teachers and other service providers. *E.g.* the Kobe-Osaka region of Japan is thickly populated because of the presence of a number of industries.

C) Socio - Cultural Factors: Religion, language, political unrest and government policis influenced the world population.

(i) **Religious:** Some places attract more people because they have religious or cultural significance. *E.g.* in USA people of different nationalities prefer their own regions where common culture and traditions are present.

(ii) Political unrest and wars: In the same way – people tend to move away from places where there is social and political unrest. E.g. refugees from Ethiopia, Sudan, Sri Lanka have moved out from their own countries.

(iii) Government policies: Many a times governments offer incentives to people to live in sparsely populated areas or move away from overcrowded places.

4. Explain the components responsible for population growth in the world.

Ans. There are three factors responsible for population change.

1. <u>Birth Rate</u>: If the births exceed deaths, within a given year there will be a net population increase.

2. <u>Death rate</u>: If the death exceeds births, within a given year there will be a net population decrease.

3. <u>Migration</u>: The permanent or semi-permanent change of a person's place of residence is called migration. <u>Immigration</u> increases population of a place whereas <u>emigration</u> decreases population of a place.

5. Push and pull factors of migration.

People migrate for better economic and social life. The factors affecting migration are divided into two groups-

A. Push Factors

i) Unemployment

ii) Low living conditions

iii) political unrest

iv) adverse climate

v) Natural disasters like flood, earthquake etc.

vi) Epidemics and famine

vii)Socio-economic backwardness.

B. Pull Factors

i) Better work opportunities

ii) Good living conditions

iii) Peace and stability

iv) Favorable climate

v) Safety of life and property

vi)Various means of entertainment

vii)Technological development

6. Science and technology helped in the population growth.

i) In 19th century due to **scientific and technological advancements** in transportation, sanitation, medical advancements, introduction of biotechnology the world population grew very rapidly.

ii) Safty features in vehicles reduced the death rates.

iii) Vecaninations secured life during pandemic.

7. Define the term Demographic Theory.

a) This theory describes and predicts the future population of any area.

b) The theory tells us that population of any region changes from high births and high deaths to low births and low deaths as society progresses from rural agricultural and illiterate to urban industrial and literate society.

c) These changes occur in stages which are collectively known as the **demographic cycle**.

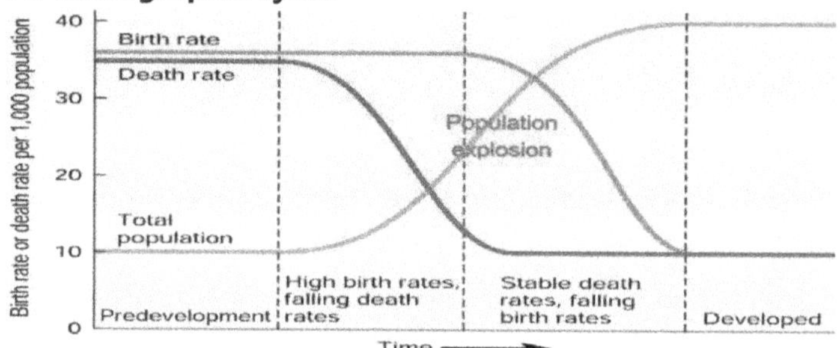

8. Describe the three-stage model of Demographic Transition Theory.

As a country changes from a rural society into an urban society there are changes in its demographic trends. These changes are represented in three stages, they are:

1. **Primitive Demographic growth**:

   a) In this stage the birth and death rates are high because people reproduce more to compensate for the deaths due to epidemics and variable food supply.

   b) Life expectancy is low.

   c) The population growth rate is slow.

   d) Most of the people are engaged in agriculture where large families are an asset.

   e) People are mostly illiterate and have low levels of technology.

   f) Two hundred years ago all the countries of the world were in this stage. It is basically found in primitive agriculture dominated countries.

2. **Expanding or youthful demographic**:
   a) In this stage birth rate remains high.
   b) Death rate decline due to technological advancements in health and improvements in sanitation conditions.
   c) Because of this gap between death and birth rate the net addition to population is high and the population growth is rapid.

3. **Late expanding demographic**:
   a) In this stage the birth and death rates declines.
   b) The population becomes urbanised, literate and has high technical knowhow and deliberately controls the family size.
   c) The population is either stable or grows slowly.

9. **Population control measures.**
   i) family planning
   ii) Propaganda
   iii) Easy availability of contraceptives
   iv) Tax incentives for large families
   v) Women's education and employment
   vi) Increase in health-medical facilities
   vii) Population Policy and Compliance
   viii) Public awareness

<u>Objectives</u>

1. In the context of which continent, George B. Cressey has said "..............in which very few people live in many places and many people live in less places".
   a) Africa   b) North America
   c) Asia   d) Europe

2. In which continent is the highest population density found?
   a) Africa   b) Europe
   c) North America   d) Asia

3. What is the actual growth of population?
   a) Birth rate - Death rate
   b) Birth rate - Death rate + Immigration
   c) Birth rate – Death rate + Immigration - Emigration
   d) Birth rate – Death rate - Emigration

4. Which continent has the highest population growth rate?
   a) Australia   b) Africa
   c) Europe   d) Asia

5. Which of the following is a densely populated area? (CBSE – 2023)
   a) Himalayan region
   b) Osaka-Kobe region of Japan
   c) Siberian region of Russia
   d) Central Chile

6. Which is the most important factor responsible for the high population density in the Katanga-Zambia Plateau located in Africa?
   a) Availability of copper in abundance
   b) Availability of forest resources
   c) Close social relations
   d) Natural beauty

7. Which of the following countries has the least population? (CBSE-2023)
   a) Mexico   b) Nigeria
   c) Russia   d) Bangladesh

8. Which of the following characteristics is not related to the first stage of the demographic transition theory?
   a) High birth and death rates
   b) Slow population growth
   c) High technology development
   d) Primary activities

Answers. 1-c, 2-d, 3-c, 4-b, 5-b, 6-a, 7-a, 8-c

CHAPTER 3 - HUMAN DEVELOPMENT

1. **Explain three differences between the growth and development.**

    Both growth and development refers to changes over a period of time. But they differ in following ways:

    a) Growth is quantitative where as the development is qualitative.

    b) Growth is value neutral which means that it can be either positive or negative where as development is always positive.

    c) Development occurs when positive growth takes place and when there is a positive change in quality. However, positive growth does not always lead to development.

2. **Explain the concept of Human development.**

    a) The concept of human development was introduced by Dr. Mahbub-ul-Haq. He described human development as development that enlarges people's choices and improves their lives.

    b) People are central to all development under this concept. The basic goal of human development is to create conditions where people can live meaningful lives.

    c) A meaningful life is not just a long one. It must be a life with some purpose. This means that people must be healthy, be able to develop their talents, participate in society and be free to achieve their goals.

3. **What are the three basic aspects of human development?**

    The three aspects of human development are:

    a) **Access to health**: Leading a long and healthy life,

    b) **Access to education**: being able to gain knowledge and

    c) **Access to resources**: having enough means to be able to live a decent life.

4. **Why human development aspects are important?**
   a) Building people's capabilities in these areas of health, education and resources is important in enlarging their choices.
   b) If people do not have capabilities in these areas, their choices also get limited.
   c) An uneducated child cannot make the choice to be a doctor because her choice has got limited by his lack of education.
   d) Similarly, very often poor people cannot choose to take medical treatment for disease because their choice is limited by their lack of resources (money).

5. **Explain the four pillars of human development.**
   The idea of human development is supported by the four pillars of **equity, sustainability, productivity** and **empowerment**.
   A) **Equity** refers to making equal access to opportunities available to everybody. The opportunities available to people must be equal irrespective of their gender, race, income and caste.
   B) **Sustainability** means continuity in the availability of opportunities. Each generation must have the same opportunities. All resources must be use keeping in mind the future. Misuse of any of these resources will lead to fewer opportunities for future generations.
   C) **Productivity** means the human-labour productivity must be constantly enriched by building capabilities in people. Efforts made to increase their knowledge, or provide better health facilities ultimately leads to better work efficiency.
   D) **Empowerment** means to have the power to make choices. Such power comes from increasing freedom and capability. Good governance and people-oriented policies are required to empower people. The empowerment of socially and economically disadvantaged groups is of special importance.

6. **Explain four different approaches of achieving human development.**

   Important approaches of human development are:

   A) **The income approach**: This is one of the oldest approaches. Human development is linked to income. The idea is that the level of income reflects the level of freedom an individual enjoys. Higher the level of income, the higher is the level of human development.

   B) **The welfare approach**: Human development is linked to government expenditure on welfare. The idea is that the level of expenditure reflects the level human development. Higher the level government expenditure on welfare, the higher is the level of human development.

   C) **Minimum needs approach**: This approach was initially proposed by the International Labour Organisation (ILO). Six basic needs i.e.: health, education, food, water supply, sanitation, and housing were identified. Higher the provision on basic needs, the higher is the level of human development.

   D) **Capabilities approach:** This approach is associated with Prof. Amartya Sen. Building human capabilities in the areas of health, education and access to resources is the key to increasing human development.

7. **What is human development index and explain the three indicators used to measure the level of human development in a region?**

   Human development index is a key of measuring the quality of life and human well-being. It is developed by United Nation Development Programme (UNDP). It is a composite index of the following indicators:

   a) **Access to health**: The indicator chosen to measure health is the life expectancy at birth. A higher life expectancy means that people have a greater chance of living longer and healthier lives.

b) **Access to education**: The indicator chosen to measure education is the adult literacy rate and the gross enrolment ratio. These two shows how easy or difficult it is to access knowledge in a particular country.

c) **Access to resources**: Access to resources is measured in terms of purchasing power (in India Rupees). If the people of any region has high purchasing power it means they have enough means to be able to live a decent life.

8. **What is Human Poverty Index? Mention the four indicators used to measure this index.**

The human poverty index is constructed by UNDP which is used to measure the **shortfall** in human development. It is a non-income measure. The four indicators used to measure it are:

a) The probability of not surviving till the age of 40,
b) The adult illiteracy rate,
c) The number of people who do not have access to clean water
d) The number of small children who are underweight.

9. **State the three differences between Human Development Index and Human Poverty Index.**

Both of these index measures human development in a region. Together these indexes give an accurate picture of human development situation in a country. But they differ on following points:

a. The human development index measures **attainments** in human development whereas the human poverty index measures the **shortfall** in human development.
b. Human development index (HDI) does not say anything about the distribution whereas the human poverty index (HPI) measures the levels of distribution of education, health and resources.

c. HDI is an income measure whereas HPI is a non-income measure.

d. The human poverty index is more revealing than the human development index.

10. **Mention some other ways of measuring human development in a country.**

    The ways to measure human development are constantly being refined and new ways of capturing different elements of human development are being researched. Some of them are-

a. Political Freedom Index: Democratic country gives political freedom which in turn influences the human development.

b. Corruption Index

c. Gross National Happiness

11. **Explain "Gross National Happiness".**

    1. Bhutan has declared Gross National Happiness as the official measure of the country's progress.

    2. Bhutan has given more importance to its environment or cultural and spiritual life than other aspects like material progress, technological development etc.

    3. The happiness index has been adopted keeping in mind the possible harm caused by material progress and technological development.

    4. It means that material progress should not be made at the cost of happiness.

    5. Gross National Happiness encourages us to think about the spiritual, material and qualitative aspects of development.

12. How countries are classified on the basis of the human development?

The scores attained by a country is important basis of classifying countries into different groups.

a. Countries with High index value
i. They have score of 0.8 and above.
ii. They are Norway, Iceland, Australia, Luxembourg and Canada.
iii. Countries with higher human development are those where a lot of investment in the social sector has taken place.
iv. Government of these countries has made a higher investment in people and provided good governance.
v. Many of these countries have been the former imperial powers.
vi. Social diversity in these countries is not very high.

b. Countries with Medium Index Value
i. They have scores between 0.500 to 0.799.
ii. Most of these countries have emerged in the period after the Second World War.
iii. Some countries from this group were former colonies while many others have emerged after the break up of the erstwhile Soviet Union in 1990.
iv. Many of these countries have been rapidly improving their human development score by adopting more people-oriented policies and reducing social discrimination.
v. Most of these countries have a much higher social diversity than the countries with higher human development scores.
vi. Many in this group have faced political instability and social uprisings at some point of time in their recent history.

c. Countries with Low Index Value
i. As many as 32 countries record low levels of human development.
ii. A large proportion of these are small countries which have been going through political turmoil and social instability in the form of civil war, famine or a high incidence of diseases.

Objectives

1. What was the rank of India according to HDI 2023?
   a) 126th   b) 130th   c) 134th   d) 135th

2. Which of the following best describes development?
   a) Increase in size
   b) Positive change in quality
   c) Stability in size
   d) Simple change in quality

3. The concept of human development is the contribution of which of the following scholars?
   a) Prof. Amartya Sen
   b) Dr. Mehboob-ul-Haq
   c) Alan C. Semple
   d) Ratzel

4. In which approach of human development, emphasis is laid on the provision of basic needs of defined classes?
   a) Income approach
   b) Welfare approach
   c) Basic needs approach
   d) Capability approach

5. Prof. According to Amartya Sen, which is the main objective of development?
   a) Increase in equality
   b) Increase in freedom
   c) Increase in democracy
   d) Increase in brotherhood

6. How many groups have the countries been divided into on the basis of human development score?
   a) 2
   b) 3
   c) 4
   d) 6

7. Which one is not an approach to human development?
   a) Income approach
   b) Welfare approach
   c) Basic needs approach
   d) Empowerment approach

8. Which one of the following is not an index of HDI?
   a) Health
   b) Education
   c) Access to resources
   d) Happiness

9. Which score is used for HDI?
   a) 0-1
   b) 1-10
   c) 0-10
   d) 10-20

10. How many minimum requirements has been proposed by ILO?
    a) 3
    b) 4
    c) 5
    d) 6

11. Which one of the following is not a minimum requirement according to ILO?
    a) Health
    b) Housing
    c) Water supply
    d) Transport

12. Since which year UNDP has been publishing Human Development Report every year?

    a) 1990   b) 1980   c) 1995   d) 2000

13. Gross National Happiness Index is measured by which country?

    a) Nepal   b) Sri Lanka   c) Maldives   d) Bhutan

14. Which country comes under "middle level of human development"?

    a) Singapore   b) Canada   c) India   d) Denmark

15. Assertion: Growth and development refer to changes that occur over a period of time.
    Reason: Development means qualitative change which is always positive.
a) Both A and R are true and R is the correct explanation of A.
b) Both A and R are true but R is not the correct explanation of A.
c) A is true but R is false.
d) A is false but R is true.

16. The combined observation of which two measures of human development presents a true picture of the state of human development in a country?
a) Human Development Index and Corruption Index
b) Human Poverty Index and Corruption Index
c) Gross National Happiness and Political Freedom Index
d) Human Development Index and Human Poverty Index

17. What weightage is given to each indicator in the Human Development Index?
    a) 1/2   b) 1/3   c) 1/4   d) 100%

18. According to the Human Development Report 2020, which of the following countries is the group of countries with top index-
a) Hong Kong, Norway, Ireland, Switzerland
b) Ireland, Norway, Hong Kong, , Switzerland
c) Norway, Switzerland, Hong Kong, Ireland
d) Norway, Ireland, Switzerland, Hong Kong

Answers- 1-c, 2-b, 3-b, 4-c, 5-b, 6-c, 7-d, 8-d, 9-a, 10-d, 11-d, 12-a, 13-d, 14-c, 15-b, 16-d, 17-b, 18-d

CHAPTER 4 - PRIMARY ACTIVITIES

1. **Define the term economic activities.**

   Human activities which generate income are known as *economic activities.* Economic activities are broadly grouped into primary, secondary, tertiary and quaternary activities.

2. **Described four different groups/types of economic activities.**

   Economic activities are broadly grouped as Primary activities, Secondary activities, Tertiary activities and Quaternary activities.

   <u>**Primary activities**</u>: - it refers to extraction/utilization of raw materials from the earth's surface. These include hunting, gathering, pastoralism, fishing, forestry, mining and agriculture.

   <u>**Secondary activities**</u>: - it includes industries that transform raw materials into finish foods having higher value. For example manufacturing cotton textiles from raw cotton, and iron and steel from iron ore.

   <u>**Tertiary activities**</u>: - it includes all kind of services provided the people such as education, health, trade and transport.

   <u>**Quaternary activities**</u>: - it represents special kind of services, which is related to highly intellectual activities. For example research and development service, information generation, information processing and transmission.

3. **Describe the characteristics of hunters and food gatherers.**

   The characteristics of hunters and gatherers are:
   a) This activity is practised in harsh climatic conditions.
   b) eople migrate frequently in search of food.
   c) People live in small groups and have no private property.
   d) Simple implements are used for hunting.
   e) Locally available materials are used for their clothing and shelter.
   f) The yield per person is very low and little or no surplus is produced.

4. **Name the regions of hunting and gathering in the world.**

    The hunters and gatherers lives in wide variety of habitats having different climates and biological resources. It is practised in:

    a) They live in harsh climates of polar areas which include northern Canada, northern Eurasia and southern Chile;

    b) They live in tropical rain forests of Low latitude zones such as the Amazon Basin, tropical Africa, Northern fringe of Australia and the interior parts of Southeast Asia.

5. **Name two types of animal rearing.**

    Depending on geographical factors, technological development animal rearing is practised either as:

    a) Pastoral Nomadism

    b) Commercial livestock rearing.

6. **What is Nomadic herding/pastoral nomadism? Describe any four main features of it.**

    a) Nomadic herding is a subsistence activity depending on animals.

    b) The people depend on animals for food, clothing, shelter and transport.

    c) The people do not live a settled life. They move from one place to another.

    d) Each nomadic community occupies a well-defined territory.

    e) Their animals depend entirely on natural vegetation.

    f) These nomads migrate with their animals with change in seasons which is called transhumance.

    g) The social status of a person is measured by the number of cattle he possesses.

7. **Name the animals reared in areas of nomadic herding.**

    a) A wide variety of animals is kept in different regions.

    b) In tropical Africa, cattle are the most important livestock,

    c) In Sahara and Asiatic deserts, sheep, goats and camel are reared.

d) In the mountainous areas of Tibet and Andes, yak and llamas.

e) In the Arctic and sub Arctic areas, reindeer are the most important animals.

8. **Mention one important feature of each of the three broad regions/areas associated with Pastoral Nomadism in the world.**

Pastoral nomadic people live in areas of grasslands. They live in areas which are either too hot or too cold. They live in three broad regions:-

a) The largest/core region extends from Sahara desert in Africa to Mongolia and Central China. This region includes Sahara desert, Arabian deserts, Savannas of Africa, Asian mountainous and plateau regions. It is hot and dry region.

b) Tundra region in Eurasia. It is cold and dry region.

c) South West Africa and the island of Madagascar. It is a temperate region.

9. **Define Transhumance. Also give areas associated with transhumance in the world.**

The seasonal migration of people with their animals in search of pastures and water is known as transhumance. Examples of transhumance are:

a) In the mountainous regions such as the Himalaya, Gujjars migrate with their animals from the plains to the mountains in summers and from mountains to the plains in winters.

b) In tundra region these people migrate from south to north in summers and from north to south in winters.

10. **Why the numbers and areas of pastoral nomads have been decreasing?**

a) Imposition of political boundaries: - Now they can not move freely in their regions due to formation of different countries.

b) New settlement plans by different countries: - Many countries have used their grazing lands for resettlement colonies and agriculture.

11. What is commercial livestock rearing? Describe the main features of Commercial Livestock Rearing (Ranching).

The capital intensive and organised rearing of animals on scientific lines is called commercial livestock rearing.

The main features of Commercial Livestock rearing are:

a) It is practised in permanent ranches.

b) The rearing of animals is being undertaken scientifically.

c) Fodder crops and grasses are cultivated to feed the animals.

d) Special breeds of animals are reared to give maximum yields of milk and meat.

e) Great emphasis is given on genetic improvement, disease control and health care of animals.

f) Every activity is carried out mechanically.

g) It is mostly practised in developed countries such as New Zealand, Australia, Argentina and United States of America.

12. What are permanent ranches?

Ranches are large areas of pastures. These ranches are divided into a number of parcels which are fenced. When the grass of one parcel is grazed, animals are moved to another parcel. The number of animals in a ranch is kept according to the carrying capacity of pasture.

13. What are agricultural systems? How are they classified?

Different types of agriculture practised under different physical and socio-economic conditions are called agricultural systems.

They are classified on the basis of:

a) Methods of farming,

b) Type of crops grown

c) Type of livestock kept.

14. **Distinguish between subsistence agriculture and commercial agriculture.**

    The agriculture systems of the world are grouped into subsistence agriculture and commercial agriculture. The differences between the two are:

    a) In the subsistence agriculture the products are consumed by the farmers' family whereas in the commercial agriculture products are sold in the market.

    b) In subsistence agriculture the farms size is small whereas in commercial agriculture it is large in size.

    c) In subsistence agriculture the yield per acre is high whereas in commercial agriculture it is low.

    d) In subsistence agriculture large number of labour is used whereas in commercial specialized machinery is used.

    e) In the subsistence agriculture system farming is very traditional whereas in commercial agriculture it is like the business enterprise.

15. **Explain the types of subsistence agriculture systems in the world.**

    There are three traditional subsistence agriculture systems in the world:

    a) **Primitive subsistence or Shifting agriculture :**

    1. It is the most primitive form of agriculture.
    2. It is mainly practiced by tribes in the tropical forest of Africa, Asia and Central America.
    3. Natural vegetations are cut and burnt to make a clearing in the forests, ash is used to increases the fertility of the soil.
    4. Fields are small and simple tools are used for cultivation.
    5. After a few years of cultivation, the soils fertility get exhausted and then the farmer move to new land and repeat the whole process of clearing the forest.
    6. Farmers return to earlier fields after 5-6 years.
    7. It is also known as slash and burn agriculture.
    8. It is prevalent in tropical regions and known by different names, e.g. **Jhuming** in North eastern states of India, **Milpa** in Central America and Mexico and **Ladang** in Indonesia and Malaysia.

b) **Intensive subsistence agriculture** :

1. It is of two types: **intensive cultivation dominated by wet paddy and intensive cultivation dominated by crops other than paddy.**
2. It is practiced in densely populated countries of monsoon Asia such as China and India.
3. Yield per acre is high due to high input of family labour.
4. Fields are small due to high density of population.
5. Most of the work is done by labour.
6. Farm yard manure is used to maintain fertility of the soil.
7. The rice, wheat, soyabean and barley are the important crops grown in this agriculture.
8. Crop specialization is not possible.
9. Multiple cropping and intercropping is common in this system.

16. Describe the main features of plantation agriculture.

a) Europeans in their colonies introduced new agriculture system known as plantation agriculture.
b) It is large-scale profit-oriented farming.
c) Main crops grown are tea, coffee, cocoa, cotton, sugarcane and rubber.
d) Large **estates** are made where single crop is grown.
e) Capital investment for construction of factories on the field.
f) Cultivation is done by Scientific methods.
g) Skilled managers and technical staff are employed.
h) Only one specialized crop is grown.
i) Estates are linked with market through good transportation.
j) Crops are exported.

17. Name important plantation crops introduced by European in different countries.

a) Cocoa and coffee plantations in West Africa established by the **French**.
b) **British** established Tea gardens in India and Sri Lanka. Rubber plantation in Malaysia. Sugarcane and Banana plantations in West Indies.
c) Coconut & Sugarcane in Philippines established by **Americans**.
d) Sugarcane plantations in Indonesia established by the **Dutch**.

18. Describe the main features of extensive commercial grain cultivation.

i. High agriculture production is achieved through efficient and more specialized agricultural machines.

ii. It is practised in interior parts of semi-arid lands.

iii. Wheat is the important crop grown in this agriculture. Other crops such as cotton, Corn, barley are also grown.

iv. The size of farm is very large therefore extensive cultivation is done.

v. The yield per acre is low but the yield per person is high due to low population density.

vi. It is practised in temperate grasslands such as **Steppes** of Europe, **Prairies** of America, **Pampas** of Argentina, **Velds** of South Africa, **Downs** of Australia.

19. Describe the main features of mixed farming.

Mixed farming is a type of farming in which cultivation of crops and raising livestock goes hand in hand. Its main features are:

i. This form of agriculture is found in the highly developed parts of the world, e.g. North-western Europe, Eastern North America, parts of Eurasia and the temperate latitudes of Southern continents.

ii. Mixed farms are moderate in size.

iii. Equal emphasis is laid on crop cultivation and animal husbandry.

iv. Fodder crops are an important component of mixed farming.

v. Crop rotation and intercropping play an important role in maintaining soil fertility.

vi. It is characterized by high capital expenditure on farm machinery and building, extensive use of chemical fertilizers and green manures.

vii. The crops associated with it are wheat, barley, oats, rye, maize, fodder and root crops.

viii. Animals like cattle, sheep, pigs and poultry provide the main income along with crops.

20. Describe the main features of dairy farming.

Dairy farming is a type of agriculture in which major emphasis is on breeding and rearing milch cattle. Its main characteristics are:

i.   It is highly capital intensive. Large investments are made on Animal sheds, storage facilities for fodder, feeding and milching machines.

ii. Special emphasis is laid on cattle breeding, health care and veterinary services.

iii. It is also highly labour intensive as it involves painstaking care in feeding and milching.

iv. There is no off-season during the year.

v.   It is practised mainly near urban and industrial market.

vi. Dairy farming development depends on transportation, refrigeration, pasteurisation and other preservation processes.

vii. There are three main regions of commercial dairy farming are:

   a. The largest is North Western Europe.

   b. Second is Canada.

   c. The third belt includes South Eastern Australia, New Zealand and Tasmania.

21. Why Dairy farming is practised mainly near urban and industrial centres?

Fresh Milk and dairy products produced in the dairy farming are easily sold in the neighbourhood urban market. Dairy products are perishable commodities therefore they have to be sold at the earliest. Urban centres are large market for the dairy products.

22. State the factors on which the development of dairy farming depends.

Dairy products are perishable commodities therefore the factors are:

Transportation: Good transport system facilitates fast movement of dairy products between farms and the market. **Refrigeration**, pasteurisation and other preservation processes increased the duration of storage of various dairy products.

23. Describe the main features of Mediterranean Agriculture.

i. Mediterranean agriculture is highly specialized commercial agriculture.

ii. It is practised in the countries on either side of the Mediterranean Sea.

iii. This region is an important supplier of citrus fruits such as grapes, oranges, olives and figs.

iv. **Viticulture** or grape cultivation is a speciality of the Mediterranean region.

v. Best quality wines are produced from high quality grapes, grapes are dried into raisins and currants.

vi. The advantage of Mediterranean agriculture is that more valuable crops such as fruits and vegetables are grown in winters when there is great demand in European and North American markets.

24. Describe the main features of market gardening and horticulture.

Cultivation of high value crops such as vegetables, flowers and fruits only for the urban markets is called horticulture and market gardening.

i. It specialize in the cultivation of high value crops such as vegetable, fruits and flowers.

ii. Crops are cultivated exclusively for the urban markets.

iii. Farms are small and are located near urban market.

iv. It is both labour and capital intensive.

v. It lays emphasis on the use of irrigation, HYV seeds, fertilisers, insecticides, greenhouses and artificial heating in colder regions.

vi. This type of agriculture is well developed in densely populated industrial areas of Europe, U.S.A. and the Mediterranean regions.

vii. Netherlands specializes in the cultivation of Flowers and horticultural crops which are flown to all major cities.

viii. Factory farming and truck farming are its two types.

25. What is Truck Farming?

The regions where farmers specialise in vegetables only, the farming is known as **truck farming**. The distance of truck farms from the market is governed by the distance that a truck can cover overnight, hence the name truck farming.

26. What is Factory Farming?

Raising of livestock, particularly poultry and cattle rearing, with heavy capital and specialization is called factory farming.

i. It is done in stalls and pens.

ii. Livestock is fed on manufactured feedstuff.

iii. It is carefully supervised against diseases.

iv. This requires heavy capital investment in terms of building, machinery for various operations, veterinary services and heating and lighting.

v. One of the important features of poultry farming and cattle rearing is breed selection and scientific breeding.

27. Name two types of farming classified on the basis of farming organization.

On the basis of farming orgainsation farming is classified into:

A. Co-operative farming

B. Collective farming.

28. Describe important features of Co-operative farming.

i. Farming is done under a cooperative society formed by a group of farmers.

ii. All farmers of the society poll in their resources voluntarily for more efficient and profitable farming.

iii. Individual farms remain intact and farming is a matter of cooperative initiative.

iv. Co-operative societies help farmers, to procure all important inputs of farming, sell the products at the most favourable terms & help in processing of quality products at cheaper rates.

v. Co-operative is successful in many western European countries like Denmark, Netherlands, Belgium, Sweden, Italy etc.

vi. In **Denmark**, the movement has been so successful that practically every farmer is a member of a co-operative.

29. Describe important features of **Collective Farming/Kolkhoz**.

a) Farming is based on social ownership of the means of production and collective labour.

b) It was introduced in erstwhile Soviet Union.

c) It was also known as **Kolkhoz** in Soviet Union.

d) The farmers pool in all their resources like land, livestock and labour.

e) Yearly targets are set by the government and the produce is also sold to the state at fixed prices.

f) Members are paid according to the nature of the work allotted to them by the farm management.

30. Give differences between co-operative farming and collective farming.

i. Co-operative farming is initiated by a group of farmers whereas collective farming is initiated by the government.

ii. In co-operative farming farmers poll in their resources, except land, voluntarily whereas in collective farming farmers poll in all resources including land.

iii. Farmers help each other voluntarily in co-operative farming whereas in collective farming farmers are allotted work by the management.

iv. In co-operative farming farmers sell their products in open market whereas in collective farming they sell the products to the government at fixed prices.

31. What are the two types of mining?

There are two types of mining:

i. **Surface mining** : it is also known as open-cast mining. Mining of minerals lying close to the surface is called surface mining. The top layers of earth are removed by digging, blasting or drilling. It is the easiest type of mining. Costs are low due to less expenditure on safety precaution and equipments. The output is large and rapid.

ii. **Underground mining** : It is also known as shaft method of mining. The extraction of minerals lying deep inside the earth is called underground mining. It is very risky and dangerous. In this kind of mining vertical and horizontal tunnels are made through which minerals are transported to the surface. It requires lifts, ventilation system, loading machines and drills.

Surface mining is a largest of all types of mining in the world.

32. Why the method of underground mining very risky?

Underground mining is very risky and every year large number of miner dies due to: -

i. Emission of poisonous gases such as methane.
ii. Accidental fires in the tunnels.
iii. Flooding due to seepage of underground water.
iv. Caving of roofs and tunnels due to water.

33. Describe the factors which influenced mining activities.

The factors which influence mining activities are:

i. **Physical factors**: the characteristics of ores such as size, depth and quality influence mining. If the mineral is found in sufficient quantity and is not found very deep, it will be mined profitably.
ii. **Economic factor**: the cost of mining, demand in the market, availability of technology and capital, supply of labour determines mining activities.

34. Why the developed economies are retreating from mining activities?

The developed countries are withdrawing from mining activities due to:

i. High labour costs.
ii. Cheap imports from developing countries.
iii. Strict environmental laws in developed countries.

35. Explain 3 reasons for the increasing use of minerals in the world.

i. Mineral production provides large export earnings for the developing countries.
ii. It provides employment to millions of miners.
iii. Minerals are used in various industries.
iv. Rising standard of living of the people has increased the demand for various minerals.

<u>Objectives</u>

1. What are the people engaged in primary work called?
   a) Blue collar workers
   b) Red collar workers
   c) White collar workers
   d) Golden collar workers

2. In which of the following regions food collection is not done?
   a) North-Canada, Eurasia and South Chile
   b) Amazon Basin
   c) Interior part of South Asia
   d) North-East USA

3. Find the corret match from the following –

Option	Region	Crop	Establisher
A	West Africa	Cocoa and Coffee	French
B	West Indies	Sugarcane & Banana	British
C	Indonesia	Sugarcane	Dutch
D	Philippines	Coconut & Sugarcane	Spanish & Americans

   a) Only A, B & C
   b) Only A, B & D
   c) Only A, C & D
   d) All are correctly matched

4. Which is not the main region of nomadic animal husbandry?
   a) Atlantic coast of North Africa-Mongolia
   b) West Europe
   c) South-West Africa-Madagascar
   d) Tundra region

5. Match the following -

Region	Major Animal Husbandry
A. Tropical Africa	I. Sheep, Goat, Camel, Horse
B. Sahara and Deserts of Asia	II. Yak, Lama
C. Tibet and Andes	III. Reindeer
D. Arctic	IV. Cow, Bull

   a) A-IV, B-I, C-II, D-III
   b) A-II, B-I, C-IV, D-III
   c) A-IV, B-III, C-II, D-I
   d) A-II, B-I, C-IV D-III

6. Wrong statement about commercial livestock farming is: (2022)
   a) Commercial livestock farming is influenced by western culture.
   b) Ranches, divided into parcels, fenced to regulate the grazing.
   c) They keep moving from one place to another according to the availability of pasture.
   d) Only one type of animal is reared.

7. In which part is primitive subsistence or shifting agriculture not done?
   - a) North-East USA
   - b) South-Central America
   - c) South-East Asia
   - d) Central Africa

8. Match the following -

Country	Primitive subsistence agriculture
A. India	I. Ladang
B. Malaysia	II. Milpa
C. Mexico	III. Jhuming

   a) A-III, B-I, C-II   b) A-II, B-I, C-III   c) A-III, B-II, C-I   d) A-II, B-I, C-III

9. What is the coffee plantation in Brazil called?
   - a) Roca
   - b) Viticulture
   - c) Fazenda
   - d) Kolkhoz

10. Which one of the following is not a plantation crop?
    - a) Cotton
    - b) Sugarcane
    - c) Banana
    - d) Maize

11. Match the Following -

Tropical grassland	country
A. Steppes	I. Australia
B. Prairies	II. South Africa
C. Pampas	III. Argentina
D. Velds	IV. Eurasia
E. Downs	V. North America

    a) A-IV, B-V, C-VIII, D-II, E-I,   b) A-V, B-IV, C-VI, D-II, E-III
    c) A-IV, B-VI, C-II, D-V, E-III,   d) A-IV, B-VI, C-V, D-II, E-I

12. Which of the following is not a region of dairy farming?
    - a) North-Western Europe
    - b) Canada
    - c) Australia-New Zealand
    - d) East Asia

13. Which of the following is not a region of mixed agriculture?
    - a) North-Eastern America
    - b) North-Western Europe
    - c) Temperate latitude parts of the Southern Continent
    - d) South-Eastern Asia

14. Grape cultivation is related to?
    - a) Floriculture
    - b) Horticulture
    - c) Viticulture
    - d) Beekeeping

15. Which is not the main region of Mediterranean agriculture?
    - a) South California
    - b) Central Chile
    - c) South-west part of South Africa
    - d) Central Africa

16. Cooperative agriculture has been most successful in ?
    a) Denmark　　b) Netherlands　　c) Belgium　　d) Sweden

17. What is collective agriculture called in Soviet Russia? (2022)
    a) Fazenda　　b) Horticulture　　c) Kolkhoz　　d) Viticulture

18. Which type of agriculture is based on the farming organization?
    a) Plantation Agriculture　　　　b) Mixed Farming
    c) Collective Farming　　　　　　d) Dairy Farming

19. Which of the following types of agriculture is a type of slash-burn agriculture?
    a) Intensive subsistence agriculture
    b) Primitive subsistence agriculture
    b) Extensive commercial grain agriculture
    d) Mixed agriculture

20. Which of the following pairs is correct? (2022)
    a) Mixed agriculture - Rice dominated agriculture
    b) Mediterranean agriculture - Citrus fruit production
    c) Intensive subsistence agriculture - Jhumming
    d) Primitive subsistence agriculture - Mechanized agriculture

21. Select the physical factor affecting mining: (2022)
    a) Demand for minerals　　　　b) Technical knowledge
    c) Development of infrastructure　　d) Size of mineral deposits

22. Select the characteristic of open mining: (2022)
    a) cheapest method of mining　　b) Lift drilling is required
    c) Ventilation system is required　　d) Labor cost is high

23. Which of the following activities comes under 'primary activity'?
    a) Animal herding　　　　　　b) Basket making
    c) Selling milk　　　　　　　　d) Sewing clothes

24. Who established rubber plantation in Malaysia?
    a) French　　b) Dutch　　c) British　　d) Spanish

25. British established which plantation agriculture in India?
    a) Coffee　　b) Rubber　　c) Sugarcane　　d) Tea

Answers: 1-b, 2-d, 3-d, 4-b, 5-a, 6-c, 7-a, 8-a, 9-c, 10-d, 11-a, 12-d, 13-d, 14-c, 15-d, 16-a, 17-c, 18-c, 19-b, 20-b, 21-d, 22-a, 23-a, 24-c, 25-d

CHAPTER 5 - SECONDARY ACTIVITIES

1. **What are secondary activities?**

   Activities which add value to natural resources and transform them into valuable products is called secondary activities.

2. **What is manufacturing?**

   a) Manufacturing refers to mass production of all/any kinds of identical goods with the use of power, specialised labour and a factory.

   b) It transforms raw materials into finished goods of high value. It is done in either by hand or power driven machinery.

   c) Industry refers to simple processing of natural raw materials. The production techniques are less complicated.

3. **Describe the characteristics of modern large-scale manufacturing.**

   Modern manufacturing industries have following characteristics:

   a) **Specialisation of skills & methods of production**: Modern manufacturing involves mass production of identical products in large quantities. Each worker performs only one task repeatedly.

   b) **Mechanisation:**

   Production is done with the help of gadgets and automatic machines which are computer controlled.

   c) **Technological Innovation:**

   New methods of production are innovated/researched and used for quality control, reducing waste and inefficiency, and controlling pollution.

   d) **Organisational Structure and Stratification:**

   The Organization of business is large which consists of CEO's, Managers, executives, workers. Each one performs a specialized task.

4. **Explain the factors which influence the location of industries in the world.**

   Industries maximize profits by reducing costs. Therefore industries are located where the costs are minimum. Some factors operate together to determine industrial location.

   The factors influencing are:

   a) **Access to Market:**
   i. Industries are located in areas/regions which have high density of population and high purchasing power. These areas provide large market.
   ii. Industries are less in remote areas inhabited by a few people. Whereas, in developed regions of Europe, North America, Japan and Australia industries are more because they provide large global markets and the purchasing power of the people is very high.
   iii. The densely populated regions of South and South-east Asia also provide large markets, thus industries are more.

   b) **Access to Raw Material:**
   i. Industries are located where the raw material is cheap and easy to transport.
   ii. Steel, sugar, and cement Industries are based on cheap, bulky and weight-losing material (ores) therefore they are located close to the sources of raw material.
   iii. Agro-processing and dairy Industries are located close to farms or dairy because the raw material is perishable.

   c) **Access to Labour Supply:**
   i. Some industries require skilled labour therefore they are located near urban-educational centres where skilled labour is easily available.

   d) *Access to Sources of Energy:*
   i. Industries which use more power are located close to the energy source, such as the **aluminium** industry.

   e) **Access to Transportation and Communication Facilities:**
   i. Speedy and efficient transport and communication facilities reduce the cost of transport and management.

ii.   Industries are attracted in regions having good transport and communication facilities.

iii.   Western Europe and eastern North America have a high numbers of industries.

f) Government Policy:

i.   Some times industries are located under Government policy of 'regional balance' & economic development.

g) Access to Agglomeration Economies/Links between Industries:

i.   Many industries benefit from nearness to a leader-industry and other industries.

ii.   These benefits are termed as agglomeration economies. Savings are derived from the linkages which exist between different industries.

5. **Explain three groups of industries classified on the basis of their size.**

   On the basis of capital investment, number of workers and volume of production industries are classified as:

A. Cottage or household industries:

a) It is the smallest manufacturing unit.

b) Family members produce goods within their homes.

c) They use locally available raw-material and sell their products in the local markets.

d) They use simple tools devised by them to produce goods.

e) Foodstuff, fabrics, shoes, pottery, furniture, mats, etc.

B. Small scale industries:

a) The place of manufacturing is outside the home/cottage.

b) This type of manufacturing use simple power-driven machines and semi-skilled labour to produce goods.

c) Raw material is obtained from locally.

d) The industries are larger in size than the cottage industries.

e) Products are sold beyond local markets.

f) They provide employments to large number of people.

g) E.g. toys, furniture, edible oil, and leather goods.

C. Large scale industries:
   a) These are heavy and capital-intensive industries.
   b) They use automatic machines and large number of people to produce goods.
   c) The products are sold in national or international markets.
   d) Emphasis is given on quality control and production specialization.
   e) Raw material is obtained from large areas.
   f) Production is on large scale.

6. **Explain two groups of industries classified on the basis of their product.**

   On the basis of output/product, industries are classified as:

   i. **Basic industries**: Industries whose products are used to produce other goods by using them as raw materials are called basic industries. For example, iron and steel industry produce steel which is used by other industries as a raw material to produce machines.

   ii. **Consumer goods industries**: industries which produce goods for direct consumption such as tea, bread, soap and television are known as consumer goods industries.

7. **Explain the groups of industries classified on the basis of their inputs.**

   On the basis of inputs/raw material, industries are classified as:

   A. Agro-based industries:
   i. Industries which utilize agriculture products as raw materials and produce goods such as cotton textile, tea, sugar and vegetable oil are called agro based industries.
   ii. Major agro-processing industries are food processing, sugar, pickles, fruits juices, beverages (tea, coffee and cocoa), spices and oils fats and textiles, rubber, etc.

   B. Forest based industries:
   i. These industries utilize Forest products as raw material.
   ii. For example paper, furniture industry, lac industries.

C. **Mineral based industries:**
   i. These industries use minerals as raw materials.
   ii. There are different mineral based industries, for example ferrous (iron) industries which uses metals which have iron content such as iron and steel industry,
   iii. Nonferrous industries which uses metals which do not have iron content such as aluminium industry,
   iv. Non-metallic industries which uses non-metals such as cement industries.

D. **Chemical industries**
   i. This industry uses chemicals as raw materials.
   ii. For example: Mineral oil is used to produce petroleum products, **Salt**, sulphur industries, Plastics industries.

7. Explain the groups of industries classified on the basis of their ownership.

On the basis of ownership, industries are classified as:

i. **Public industries**: when the ownership and management of an industry is in the hands of the State, it is called public sector industry.

ii. **Private sector industries**: industries owned and managed by an individual or a corporate body belongs to private sector. Individuals invest their own capital and they manage these industries themselves.

iii. **Joint sector industries**: industries owned and managed jointly by the State and private individuals belong to join sector industries.

8. State any five important features of high-tech industries.

High-tech or modern industries have following important features:

a) Highly skilled specialist professional (white collar) workers make up a large share of the total workforce.

b) Scientific and engineering products are manufacture through intensive research and development.

    c) Robotics, computer-aided design (CAD), electronic controls are notable examples of a high-tech industry.

    d) The office & plant buildings are modern & neatly spaced.

    e) Planned business parks for high-tech industries have been set up.

9. What are technopolies and Planned Business Parks?

Technopolies- High-tech industries which are regionally concentrated, self-sustained and highly specialised are called technopolies. The Silicon Valley near San Francisco and Silicon Forest near Seattle are examples of technopolies.

Planned Business Parks - Areas that are planned for the purpose of industrial development and contain offices and light industry rather than heavy industry.

10. What are Agro-Factories?

    a) Agro-business is a type of commercial agriculture which is done on an industrial scale. It is usually financed by a business whose main interest is outside agriculture.

    b) Agro-businesses are larger in size than farms, mechanized, dependent on chemicals and have a good structure.

    c) These are called 'agro-factories'.

11. Foot Loose Industries-

i) Located in a wide variety of places.

ii) Do not depend on raw material.

iii) Production can be in small quantities.

iv) Less labour is required.

v) Do not spread pollution.

vi) Requires a better road network.

12. Why are high technology industries developing in the periphery of metros?

    a) Scientific and engineering products are produced through the use of intensive research and development.

    b) White collar workers predominate and modern offices and laboratories are required.

c) Conditions for building business are available in metros.

d) Development of high technology industry has been made possible in most of the metropolitan areas due to transport, security, internet facility etc.

Objectives

1. Secondary activities are not related to?
   a) Management b) Manufacturing c) Processing d) Infrastructure

2. Corn belt is found in which country?
   a) America   b) India   c) Nigeria   d) Brazil

3. Which of the following industries is set up very close to the energy source?
   a) Iron and Steel b) Aluminium c) Dairy Industry d) Free Industry

4. Which of the following is not an example of size based industry?
   a) Large Scale Industry   b) Cooperative Sector
   c) Cottage Industry   d) Small Scale Industry

5. Which city of India is called the 'Silicon Valley of India'?
   a) Hyderabad b) Chennai c) Bengaluru d) Mumbai High

6. Which one of the following is not correctly matched?
   a) Rubber industry – Agriculture based
   b) Leather industry – Animal based
   c) Salt industry – Mineral based
   d) Lac industry – Forest based

7. Which one of the following is not a characteristic of cottage industry? (2023)
   a) Smallest unit of manufacturing   b) Use of simple tools
   c) Construction site outside home   d) Use of local raw material

8. Which one of the following types of industries produces raw materials for other industries?
   (a) Cottage Industries   (c) Basic Industries
   (b) Small-scale Industries   (d) Footloose Industries

Answers: 1-a, 2-a, 3-b, 4-b, 5-c, 6-c, 7-c, 8-c

CHAPTER 6 - TERTIARY & QUATERNARY ACTIVITIES

1. **What are tertiary activities?**

   Commercial output and exchange of services are called tertiary activities. Tertiary activities include both production and exchange. All Services which require special skills of theoretical knowledge and practical training and are provided in exchange of payments is included in tertiary sector.

2. **Give differences between tertiary activities and secondary activities.**

   The main differences between them are:

   a) Services rely more heavily on specialised skills, experience and knowledge of the workers whereas secondary activities rely on the production techniques, machinery and factory processes.

   b) Tertiary activities involve the commercial output of services whereas secondary activities involve the production of tangible goods.

   c) Tertiary activities are not directly involved in the processing of physical raw materials.

3. **What are trading centres? Name two types of trading centres.**

   A place where trading of goods and services takes place is known as trading centre. It can be at local level or international level, urban or rural areas. Trading centres may be divided into rural and urban marketing centres.

4. **Distinguish between rural marketing centres and urban marketing centres.**

   Both of the marketing centres differ from each other:

   a) Rural marketing centres provide facility to nearby settlements whereas urban marketing centres provide facility to wide services to large areas.

   b) Rural centres are mostly rudimentary type whereas urban centres offer specialised services.

c) Personal and professional services are undeveloped in rural centres whereas they are highly developed in urban centres.

d) Rural marketing centres acts as a local collecting and distributing centres whereas urban marketing centres provide services beyond cities at national or international levels.

5. **Distinguish between wholesale and retail trading services.**
   Retail trading services:
   a) This is the business activity concerned with the sale of goods directly to the consumers.
   b) Retail trading is done through fixed **Stores**- large shops.
   c) It is also done through **Non-stores**- Street peddling, door-to-door, mail-order, telephone, automatic vending machines and internet.

   Wholesale trading services:
   a) This is the business activity concerned with the bulk selling of goods through merchants and supply-houses.
   b) Wholesalers acts as intermediaries between retail stores and manufacturers.
   c) Wholesalers also give credit to retail stores.

6. **Explain the significance of transport and communication services.**
   a) A Transport and communication service has helped in the development of modern economies.
   b) Transport service is used to physically carry persons, manufactured goods, and property from one location to another.
   c) It is an organised industry which satisfies man's basic need of mobility.
   d) Speedy and efficient transport systems assist in the production, distribution and consumption of goods.
   e) At every stage, the value of the material is significantly enhanced by transportation.

7. **State three ways of measuring transport distance.**

Transport distance is measured by:

Km distance: it is the actual distance of route length.

Time distance: it is the time taken to travel on a particular route.

Cost distance: it is the expense of travelling on a route.

8. **Explain the factors which affect the transport services.**

   a) In selecting the **mode of transport**, time and cost distance, is the determining factor.

   b) **Demand** for transport is influenced by the size of population. The larger the population size, the greater is the demand for transport.

   c) **Routes** depend on Location of cities, towns, villages, industrial centres and raw materials, Pattern of trade between them, Nature of the landscape between them, Type of climate, Funds available for overcoming obstacles along the length of the route.

9. **What are communication services? Explain the factors on which communication services depends.**

   Activities related to transmission of words and massages, ideas and facts are termed as communication services. It depends on:

   a) Communication services depend on transport network. Where the transport network is efficient, communications are easily spread.

   b) Certain developments, such as mobile telephony and satellites, have made communications independent of transport.

   c) Due to the cheapness of the transport systems very large volumes of mail continue to be handled by post offices all over the world.

10. **Name different types of communication services.**

    1. Means of transportation: include road, rail and air services.

    2. Telecommunication: include telephone and mobile.

    3. Audio visual: include mass media such as films, radio, T.V., Newspaper and Magazines.

11. **Describe different types of services.**

Services occur at many different levels.

A. Some are provided to industry, some to people; and some to both industry and people, e.g. the transport systems.

B. Low-order services, such as grocery shops and laundries, are more common and widespread than high-order services or more specialised ones like those of accountants, consultants and physicians.

C. Services provided to individual consumers. For example the gardener, the launderers and the barber do primarily physical labour. Teacher, lawyers, physicians, musicians and others perform mental labour.

D. Regulated or formal services such as Making and maintaining highways and bridges, maintaining fire fighting departments and supplying education and customer-care, transport, telecommunication, energy and water supply.

E. Professional services are primarily health care, engineering, law and management.

F. Recreational and entertainment services.

12. **What are informal or non-formal services?**

Some personal services, made available to the people to facilitate their work in daily life, are unorganized or unregulated such as domestic services of housekeepers, cooks, and gardeners. The workers employed in these services are migrants from rural areas and are unskilled. One such example in India is Mumbai's **Dabbawala** (Tiffin) service provided to about 1, 75, 000 customers all over the city.

13. **Name the single largest tertiary activity in the world. Give facts in support of your answer.**

Tourism is travel undertaken for purposes of recreation rather than business. It has become the world's single largest tertiary activity. The facts are:

i.   It provides jobs to about 250 million people.

ii. It has provided total revenue 40 per cent of the total GDP.

iii. Many local persons are employed to provide services like accommodation, meals, transport, entertainment and special shops serving the tourists.

iv. Tourism promotes the growth of infrastructure industries, retail trading, and craft industries.

v. In some regions tourism provide source of income all year.

14. Explain the factors which affects the development of tourism in the world.

i. With the improvement in the standard of living the demand for holidays has increased.

ii. With increased leisure time many more people go on holidays for leisure.

iii. New tourist destination has been opened up recently.

iv. Improvement in road transport facilities has made travel easier

v. More significant in recent years has been the expansion in air transport. For example, air travel allows one to travel anywhere in the world in a few hours of flying time from their homes.

vi. The advent of package holidays reduced the costs of travel.

15. Mention some of the important tourist attractions in the world.

Tourists attract to places which have following features:

A. **Climate***:* Most people from colder regions get attracted to warm, sunny weather for beach holidays. This is one of the main reasons for the importance of tourism in Southern Europe and the Mediterranean lands because it offers higher temperatures and long hours of sunshine.

B. **Landscape***:* Many people like to spend their holidays in mountains, lakes, spectacular sea coasts and landscapes not completely altered by man.

C. **History and Art**: People visit ancient or picturesque towns and archaeological sites, and enjoy exploring castles, palaces and churches.

D. **Culture and Economy**: These attract tourists with a liking for experiencing ethnic and local customs.

16. **What are quaternary activities? State important features of quaternary activities?**

    The **quaternary activities** refer to intellectual occupations which are advance and specialised such as thinking, research and developing new ideas. Its important features are:

a. These services are advance and specialized economic activities.

b. These services concern mainly with information processing, research and development.

c. These services offer high income.

d. These services are mainly concentrated in developed countries and growing fast.

e. It involves specialized knowledge, technical skills, and administrative competence.

f. It belongs to service sector that is knowledge oriented (KPO).

g. Like some of the tertiary functions, quaternary activities can also be outsourced.

h. They are not tied to resources, affected by the environment, or necessarily localised by market.

i. Important occupations belonging to quaternary activities are: mutual fund managers, tax consultants, software developers, statisticians.

17. **What are quinary activities? State any four important features of quinary activities.**

    Quinary activities refer to the activities performed by the highest level of decision makers or policy makers. Its important features are:

a. It includes special and highly paid skills.

b. Services of senior business executives, government officials, research scientists, financial and legal consultants, etc. are included in it.

c. Quinary activities are services that focus on the creation, re-arrangement and interpretation of new and existing ideas, data and technologies.

18. **What is outsourcing? Explain its important features.**

    Outsourcing is giving work to an outside agency to improve efficiency and reduce costs. Outsourcing involves transferring work to overseas locations. **Its important features are**:

    a. Outsourcing has resulted in the opening up of a large number of call centres in India, China, Israel, Philippines and Costarica.

    b. It has created new jobs in these countries.

    c. Outsourcing is coming to those countries where cheap and skilled workers are available.

    d. With the work available though outsourcing, the migration in these countries may come down.

    e. Outsourcing countries are facing resistance from job-seeking youths in their respective countries.

    f. There are two types of outsourcing KPO (Knowledge processing outsourcing) and BPO (Business process outsourcing).

19. **Give three differences between KPO and BPO.**

    KPO and BPO are the part of quaternary activities. They differ under following points:

    a) The KPO industry involves more high skilled workers.

    b) It is information driven Knowledge Outsourcing whereas BPO is outsourcing of Business activities such as customer care.

    c) KPO enables companies to create additional business opportunities whereas BPO enables companies to reduce cost and increase efficiency.

    d) Examples of KPOs include research and development (R and D) activities, e-learning, business research, intellectual property (IP) research, legal profession and the banking sector.

20. **What is digital divide?**

    There are wide differences between countries and within country in the accessibility of Information and Communication Technology (ICT). This gap in accessibility of ICT is called digital divide.

Red collar   – Primary activity workers.
Blue collar   – Production workers who perform physical labour.
White collar – Salaried professionals.
Grey collar   – Who are classified as neither blue nor white collar.
Pink collar   – Usually used for female workers (jobs).
Gold collar   – Highly skilled people engaged in quinary activities.

Objectives

1. Which of the following is not related to the quinary activity?
   a) Insurance   b) Expert
   c) Consultant   d) Policy maker

2. Which of the following facilities is not included in exchange?
   a) Trade   b) Production
   c) Transportation   d) Communication

3. Lines on a map to join places equal in time taken to reach called?
   a) Isobar   b) Isotime
   c) Isotherm   d) Isochrone

4. Which of the following is not included in communication?
   a) Message   b) Thought
   c) Internet   d) Fact

5. Dabbawala service is popular in which metropolis?
   a) Delhi   b) Kolkata
   c) Mumbai   d) Chennai

6. Which is not a characteristic of periodic market?
   a) Fortnightly market   b) Fixed date and day
   c) Service to wide area   d) Fixed location

7. KPO expands to:
   a) Knowledge Processing Outsourcing
   b) Knowledge Profit Outing
   c) Knowledge Provide Outcome
   d) Knowledge People Output

8. What is the expansion of BPO?
a) Business Process Outcome
b) Business Process Outsourcing
c) Business Process Outsource
d) Business Professional Outcome

9. The characteristic of outsourcing is?
   a) Environmental pollution   b) Improving efficiency
   c) Increasing cost   d) Working only with local agency

10. Which one of the following sectors provides maximum employment in Delhi, Mumbai, Chennai and Kolkata?
    a) Primary Sector   b) Secondary Sector
    c) Tourism Sector   d) Service Sector

11. Those activities which involve high volume and level of exploration are called:
    a) Secondary activities   b) Tertiary activities
    c) Quaternary activities   d) Quinary activities

12. Which of the following belongs to the quaternary sector?
    a) Computer manufacturing   b) University teaching
    c) Paper and pulp manufacturing d) Printing of books

13. Which activity is not an example of Knowledge Processing Outsourcing (KPO)?
    a) E-learning   b) Intellectual property
    c) Information gathering   d) Legal profession

14. Which of the following is an example of inferior service?
    a) Teacher   b) Gardener
    c) Lawyer   d) Musician

15. Madikere and Coorg in Karnataka are examples of which of the following?
    a) Homestays   b) Beach Retreats
    c) Medical Tourism   d) Outsourcing

Answers: 1-a, 2-b, 3-d, 4-c, 5-c, 6-d, 7-a, 8-b, 9-b, 10-d, 11-d, 12-b, 13-c, 14-b, 15-a

CHAPTER 7 - TRANSPORT AND COMMUNICATION

1. **Explain the importance of trade, transport and communication?**
   a) They link the areas of production with areas of consumption.
   b) They reduce distance between places of natural resources, manufacturing and market.
   c) They facilitate the movement and exchange of goods and services and people.
   d) Today's world economy heavily depends on efficient trade, transport and communication.
   e) High living standard and quality of life depend on efficient transport, communication and trade.
   f) It promote cooperation and unity among scattered peoples

2. **What is the meaning of term transport?**
   It is a service for the carriage of goods and passengers from one place to other using different modes such as humans, animals and vehicles. This movement of goods and passengers take place through land, water and air therefore it has four modes namely roadways and railways, waterways, pipelines and airways.

3. **What is the meaning of term communication?**
   It means conveyance of information from the place of origin to the place of destination. Communication can be done through postal services, telephone and fax services, internet and satellites. The information is conveyed through a channel such as wires, radio waves and other frequencies.

4. **What is the meaning of trade?**
   Trade means exchange of goods and services in terms of value.

5. **Explain the three factors on which the significance of a mode of transport depends.**
   The three factors on which the significance of a mode of transport depends are: -

A. Type of goods to be transported: - if the goods which are to be carried are bulky and heavy they can be transported easily by the water ways. If the goods are of high value and perishable they are transported by airways. Liquids and gasses are transported easily by pipelines.

B. Transportation cost: - road transportation is cheaper for short distances while railways are used when the distance is long. Inter national trade is done through waterways as it is cheaper.

C. Means of transport available: - remote and hilly areas can be reached by airways as no other transportation is available. For transport of goods from ports roadways are used.

6. Describe the developments which brought revolution in land transport in the world.

In early days the humans and animals were the carriers. Revolution in land transportation came after:

a) Invention of steam engine in the eighteenth century. It resulted in the introduction of public railway lines which became the most popular and fastest form of transport in the nineteenth century. It opened up continental interiors for commercial grain farming, mining and manufacturing.

b) The invention of the internal combustion engine. The road quality and vehicles (motor cars and trucks) plying over them increased many folds.

c) Among the newer developments in land transportation are pipelines, ropeways and cableways.

d) Liquids like mineral oil, water, sludge and sewers are transported by pipelines.

7. What are the recent\latest developments in land transport?

a) Ropeways and cableways have been developed in hilly and difficult terrain.

b) Pipelines are used to transport liquids and gasses such as mineral oil, water, sludge and sewers.

8. Explain why freight transport by road is gaining importance.

  a) Road transport is the most economical for short distances as compared to railways.

  b) Roads are important than other modes of transport because it offers door to door services.

  c) They provide long distance links through highways, motorways and autobahn.

  d) Due to increase in the size of Lorries and its power, roadways can now carry large and heavy goods.

9. What are the problems/limitations of road transport?

  Road transport suffers from some limitations such as:

  a) Unmetalled roads are not effective and serviceable during the rainy season. These become unmotorable.

  b) Even the metalled ones are seriously handicapped during heavy rains and floods.

  c) The quality of roads varies greatly between countries because the construction and maintenance is very high.

  d) Many cities suffer from traffic congestion during peak hours.

10. What are highways?

  a) Highways are metalled roads connecting distant places.

  b) Such roads are constructed in a manner that vehicles could ply in an unobstructed manner.

  c) These roads are wide as much as 80 meters, smooth, and duel-carriage.

  d) Several bridges and traffic lanes are constructed for the smooth flow of traffic.

11. Describe some of important highways of the world.

  a) European ports are connected with each city through highways.

  b) In Russia, Moscow is connected by roads to the city of Vladivostak.

c) North American highways link cities of east coasts with that of west coasts.

d) Trans Canadian highway links Vancouver with St.John city.

e) Pan –American highway links cities of South America, Central America, and the United States of America.

f) Golden Quadrangle links metropolitan cities in India.

12. What are border roads? Why they are built?

a) Roads laid along international boundaries are called border roads.

b) Integrating people in remote areas with major cities.

c) Providing defence by supplying goods to military camps in border areas.

13. State the importance of railways by giving examples.

a) Railways are cheaper than roadways in carrying heavy goods.

b) They carry large number of passengers over a long distance. For e.g. in European countries railways are important mode of travel use by the people.

c) They link areas of production with areas of consumption for example railway network is dense in coffee growing areas of Brazil.

d) Railways link coastal ports cities to mining areas and inland cities. For e.g. in Chile railways links coastal ports and mining areas.

e) Commuter trains have become very popular in large cities. Such as Metro services in Delhi city.

14. Explain the factors influencing the density of rail network. Describe major regions of dense rail network in the world.

Major Rail network is found in following regions of the world:

a) The industrial regions have the highest densities of rail network in the world. Europe has one of the most dense rail networks in the world. Belgium has the highest density.

b) In Russia, railways account for about 90 per cent of the country's total transport with a very dense network in European west. Moscow is the most important station.

c) The most dense rail network is found in the highly industrialised and urbanised region of East Central U.S.A. and adjoining Canada. North America has one of the most extensive rail networks accounting for nearly 40 per cent of the world's total.

d) Australia has dense network in New South Wales. New Zealand's railways are mainly in the North Island to serve the farming areas.

e) In South America, the rail network is the most dense in two regions, namely, the Pampas of Argentina and the coffee growing region of Brazil which together account for 40 per cent of South America's total route length. Railways link coastal centres with the mining sites in the interior.

f) In Asia, rail network is the densest in the thickly populated areas of Japan, China and India. West Asia is the least developed in rail facilities because of vast deserts and sparsely populated regions.

g) In Africa continent, South Africa has dense network due to the concentration of gold, diamond and copper mining activities.

15. What are Trans-Continental Railways? Name any five important transcontinental railways in the world. Give important features of each.

Trans–continental railways run across the continent and link its two ends. They were constructed for economic and political reasons to facilitate long runs in different directions. The following are the most important of these:

1. Trans-Siberian Railway line-

a) It is from **St. Petersburg** in the west to **Vladivostak** on the Pacific Ocean in the east passing through Moscow in Russia.

b) The total length of this line is about 9332 km, longest in Asia.

c) It is double track route and electrified railway.

d) It connects Russian agro-centres, fur centres.

e) It has connecting links with many other countries. Therefore it is regionally very important.

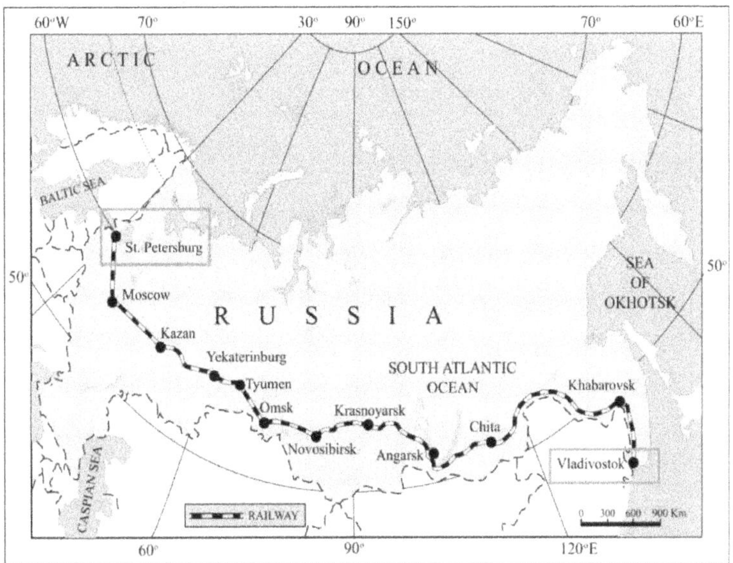

2. Trans-Canadian Pacific Railway-

a) It is in Canada from Halifax in the east to Vancouver on the west on Pacific Ocean.

b) It was constructed in 1886 & its total length is about 7050 km.

c) It gained significance because it connect industrial region of Quebec-Montreal with softwood forest region and wheat belt of the Prairies.

d) A loop line from it connects the important waterway of Great Lakes. This is the economic artery of Canada.

e) Wheat and meat are the important exports on this route.

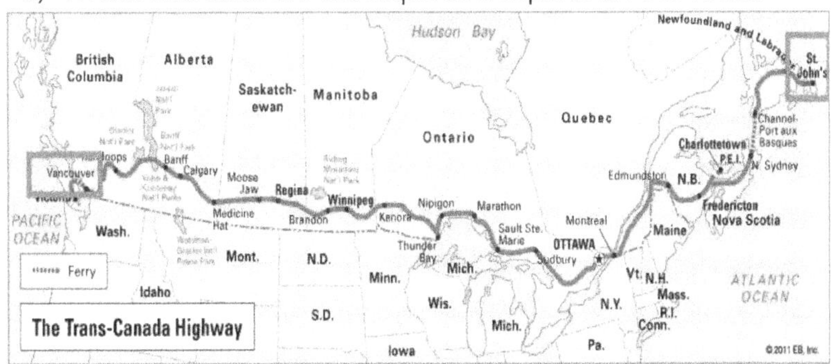

3. Australian Trans-Continental Railway –

a) It connects Sydney on the east with Perth on the west coast.

b) It runs east-west through the southern part of the Australia.

c) Constructed for the economic development of the region.

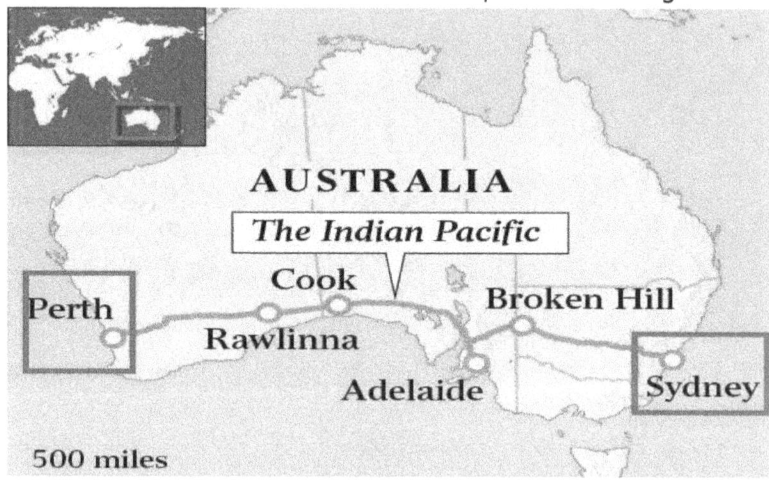

4. The Union and Pacific Railway:

a) This rail-line connects New York on the Atlantic Coast to San Francisco on the Pacific Coast.

b) The most valuable exports on this route are ores, grain, paper, chemicals and machinery.

5. The Orient Express:

a) This line runs from Paris to Istanbul.

b) The journey time from London to Istanbul by this Express is now reduced to 96 hours as against 10 days by the sea-route.

c) The chief exports on this rail-route are cheese, bacon, oats, wine, fruits, and machinery.

16. What are the four advantages of water transport?

a) It does not require route construction.

b) The oceans are linked with each other and are open with ships of various sizes.

c) It is the cheapest mode of transport as the friction of water is less than the friction of air and land.

d) It saves energy cost of transportation.

e) Heavy cargo can be easily transported by the waterways.

17. What are the advantages of ocean transport in the world?

a) It is the cheaper means of transporting goods.

b) Oceans offer free highway with no maintenance cost and can be traveled in all directions.

c) The ships are capable of carrying large loads to longer distances.

d) With improvement in its facilities such as refrigeration the efficiency of ocean transport has improved.

e) Use of containers has made cargo handling easier.

18. Which factors has improved the efficiency of ocean transport in the world?

a) Introduction of refrigerated chambers for transporting perishable goods such as fruits, vegetables, meat.

b) Development of specialized ships such as tankers for moving mineral oil and gas.

c) Development of passenger liners equipped with radar, wireless and navigation aids.

d) Use of containers has made cargo handling at ports easier.

19. Name the busiest ocean transport in the world. Why it is the most important and busiest route in the world?

1. North Atlantic route-

a) It connects the two most developed continents of the world namely USA and Europe.

b) It is the busiest route of the world because foreign trade over this route is greater than that of the rest of the world. Also called Big Trunk Route.

c) Important ports are New York, London, Lisbon, and Amsterdam. Both the coasts have highly advanced ports and harbour facilities.

2. The Mediterranean and the Indian ocean route-

a) Industrially developed countries of Europe are connected with commercial agriculture regions of south Asian & Australia through the route.

b) Europe exports machinery and industrial goods to Asian countries and Asian countries export agricultural products and raw material to Europe.

c) Important centers are Mumbai, Kochin, and Aden.

d) The volume of trade and traffic between both East and West Africa is on the increase due to the development of the rich natural resources such as gold, diamond, copper, tin, groundnut, oil palm, coffee and fruits.

3. The Cape of Good Hope-

a) It provides link between West Europe and African countries with Brazil, Argentina in South America.

b) The rich natural resources are exported to the Europe and industrial products are imported by African countries.

c) The traffic is far less on this route because of the limited development and low population in South America & Africa.

4. The North Pacific Route-

a) It links the western coasts of North America such as Vancouver, Seattle, and Portland with the ports of Asia such as Tokyo shanghai, Hong Kong.

b) All the trade converges at Honolulu.

c) Food products and manufactured goods are exported to Asia and Asia in turn exports textiles, rubber, raw materials.

20. Name two shipping canals in the world. State four features of both.

The two manmade navigation/shipping canals in the world are:

1. The Suez Canal route-

a) It is man-made waterway in Egypt which connects Port Said on Mediterranean Sea with Port Suez on the Red Sea.

b) It is the sea level canal without locks & about 160 km long and 11 to 15 m deep.

c) It was constructed in 1869.

d) It is a gateway to the Indian Ocean and reduces the distance between Western Europe and South East Asian countries by 6400 km.

e) It has helped in the development of surrounding countries such as India.

f) About 100 ships travel daily and each ship takes 10-12 hours to cross this canal. The tolls are so heavy that some find it cheaper to go by the longer Cape Route.

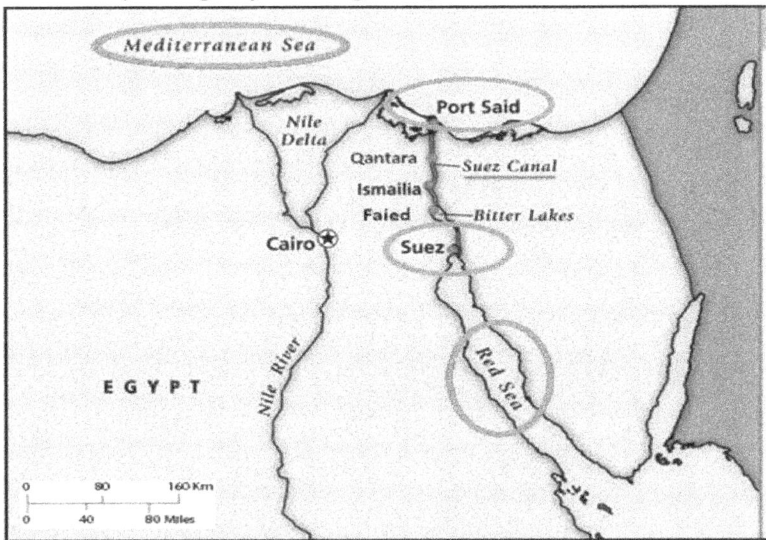

2. The Panama Canal-

a) It is man-made waterway in Panama Isthmus.

b) It connects **Colon city** on Atlantic Ocean in the east with **Panama city** on Pacific Ocean in the west.

c) It separates the land mass of N. America from S. America.

d) Provides shorter route between East Asia and W. Europe.

e) It has six lock systems. Ships cross the canal through locks.

f) The economic importance of this canal is less than that of Suez Canal. It is vital to the economies of Latin America.

g) The Canal is about 72 km. long.

h) It shortens the distance between New York and San Francisco by 13,000 km by sea.

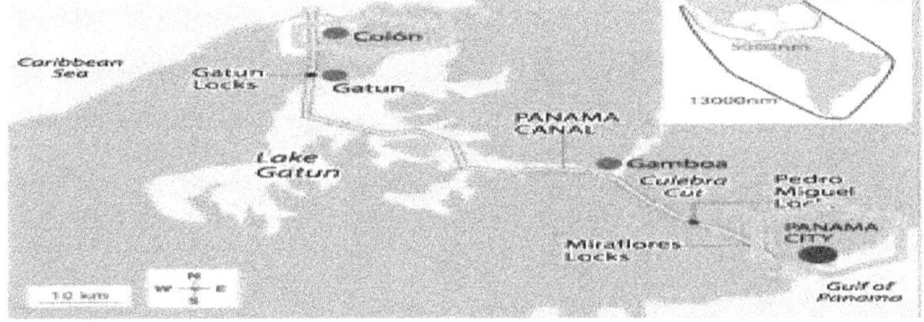

21. Explain the three factors on which the development of inland transport depends.

The inland transport depends on three factors for its development. They are:

a) Width and depth of channel: silt (sand) deposited in the river/channel bed obstructs movement of boats therefore channels having large width and deep bed is suitable for inland transport.

b) Continuity in the flow of water: lack of water due to divergence for irrigation hinders the development of inland transport.

c) Transport technology in use: poor maintenance of inland waterways and inefficient transport restricts its development.

22. Why riverways have lost its advantages in many parts of the world?

a) Competition from railways.

b) Problem of silt in rivers and canals.

c) Lack of water in the river due to diversion for irrigation.

d) Poor maintenance of river channels.

23. Mention three measures taken to improve the navigability of river channel.

Despite inherent limitations, many rivers have been modified to enhance their navigability by:

a) Dredging, removing the silt by machines from the river bed.

b) Stabilising river banks by concrete.

c) Building dams and barrages for regulating the flow of water.

24. Describe important inland waterways of the world.

Important inland waterways of the world are:

1. The Rhine Waterways:

a) Rhine River flows through Germany and the Netherlands.

b) It is navigable for 700 km from Rotterdam, Netherlands to **Basel** in Switzerland.

c) It flows through a rich coalfield and the whole basin has become a prosperous manufacturing area.

d) This waterway is the world's most heavily used.

e) It connects the industrial areas of Switzerland, Germany, France, Belgium and the Netherlands with the North Atlantic Sea Route.

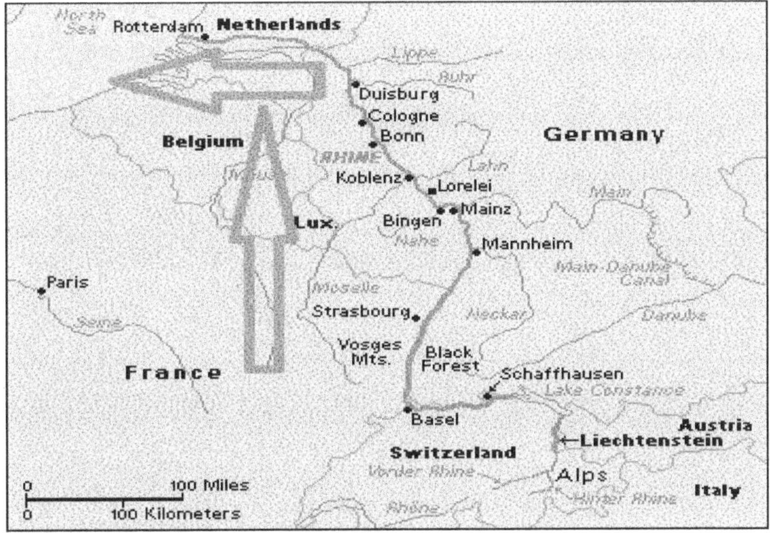

2. The Danube Waterway:

a) This important inland waterway serves Eastern Europe.

b) The Danube river rises in the Black Forest and flows eastwards through many countries.

3. The Volga Waterway:

a) The Volga is one of the most important waterways in Russia.

b) It provides a navigable waterway of 11,200 km up to the Caspian Sea.

4. The Great Lakes – St. Lawrence Seaway:

a) The Great Lakes of North America Superior, Huron Erie and Ontario are connected by Canal to form an inland waterway.

b) The estuary of St. Lawrence River, along with the Great Lakes, forms a unique commercial waterway in the northern part of North America.

c) The ports on this route like Duluth and Buffalo are equipped with all facilities of ocean ports.

d) As such large oceangoing vessels are able to navigate up the river deep inside the continent to Montreal.

e) But her goods have to be trans-shipped to smaller vessels due to the presence of rapids. Canals have been constructed up to 3.5 m deep to avoid these.

f) This has helped in the industrial and economic development of this region.

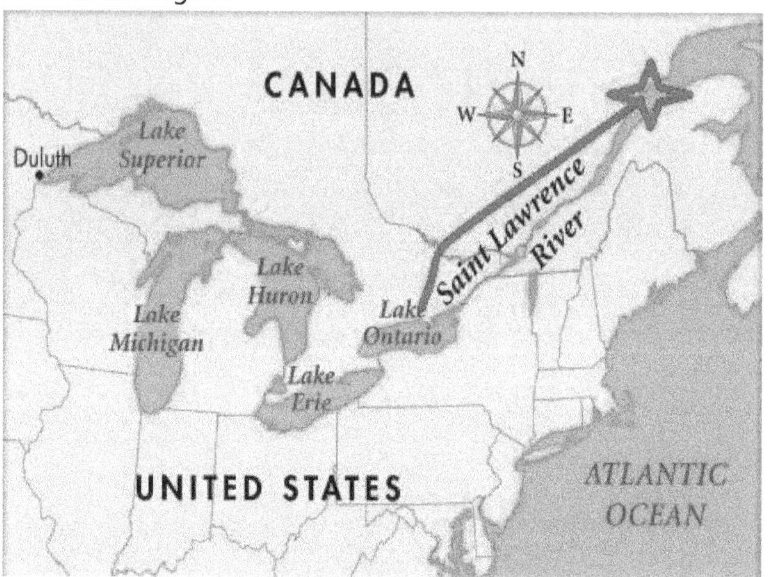

25. Explain the significance of air transport.

Air transport has brought about a connectivity revolution in the world in following ways-

a) It is the fastest mode of transport.

b) Air transport is used only for high value goods & passengers.

c) Valuable goods can be moved rapidly.

d) It is preferred for long distance travel.

e) It is the easy way to reach inaccessible areas as mountainous or inhospitable deserts.

f) In the Himalayan region, the routes are often obstructed due to landslides, avalanches or heavy snow fall.

Requirements For The Development of Air Transport

1. Airports with wide facilities have to be build.

2. The construction of airports and facilities is very costly therefore airports are built in places where the traffic is large.

3. It requires large arrangements such as hanger, fueling, landing facilities.

26. Name the major regions having dense network of airways?
   The three regions are:
   a. Western Europe: important airports are Rome, London, Berlin.
   b. Eastern United States of America: airports are New York,
   c. Southeast Asia: airports are Singapore, Bangkok.

27. Give advantages of pipelines. Why pipelines are extensively used in the world to transport oil and gas?
   a) Pipelines are used to transport liquids and gasses such as water, mineral oil and natural gas for uninterrupted flow.
   b) Cooking gas or LPG and milk (in New Zealand) is supplied through it.
   c) They are used to transport coal mixed with water.
   d) Pipelines carry mineral oil from oil fields to refineries.
   e) The famous pipeline of USA is **'Big Inch'** which carries mineral oil from Gulf of Mexico to eastern part of USA.
   f) The proposed Iran-India via Pakistan international oil and natural gas pipeline will be the longest in the world.

28. Describe the importance of communications.
   1. Telegraph has helped in the past to colonize American West.
   2. Telephone has promoted urbanization of America
   3. It has helped in spread of the industries in smaller towns.
   4. Now due to telephone many firms have their offices and branches in smaller towns.
   5. In developing countries, the use of cell phones, made possible by satellites, is important for rural connectivity.
   6. The world has converted into a **global village** because of fast and reliable means of communication.

29. What is internet and Cyberspace? State merits of internet.
   a) It is an electronic network of computer which connects million of people across the world.
   b) It is the result of digitalization of information in which the telecommunication is merged with computers.
   c) It is the largest electronic network of the world.

d) **Cyberspace** is the world of electronic computerised space. It is encompassed by the Internet with World Wide Web (www).

e) Electronic commerce is done through internet.

f) It helps in connecting to the world of knowledge from anywhere in the world.

g) It gives access to personal communication through e-mail.

30. Explain the importance of Satellite communication.

a) Satellites has brought changes in the areas of communication by reducing the time and cost of it.

b) It cost same to communicate over 500 km as it does over 5000 km. it has made long distance communication very efficient and effect.

c) Through it information on weather, weather forecasting about storm and news is collected effetely.

31. Describe how the modern communications has converted the world into global village.

a) The modern communications such as internet has expanded. Billions of people use the Internet each year.

b) Cyberspace has expanded the contemporary economic and social space of humans through e-mail, e-commerce, e-learning and e-governance.

c) Internet together with fax, television & radio will be accessible to more and more people cutting across place and time.

d) It is these modern communication systems that have made the concept of **Global Village** a reality.

<u>Objectives</u>

1. The first railway line started between in 1825?

    a) London-Birmingham   b) Stockton-Darlington

    c) Darlington-London   d) Stockton-Birmingham

2. Autobahns are popular in which country?

    a) Germany   b) France

    c) UK   d) USA

3. Which continent has the highest road density?
    a) Asia   b) Europe
    c) North America   d) South America

4. Which country has the highest rail density?
    a) Japan   b) Russia
    c) Belgium   d) France

5. Channel Tunnel connects:
    a) London-Berlin   b) Berlin-Paris
    c) Paris-London   d) Barcelona-Berlin

6. The transcontinental railway of South America connects:
    a) Buenos Aires - Valparaiso   b) St Petersburg–Vladivostok
    c) Halifax - Vancouver   d) Perth - Sydney

7. Blue Train connects which places in the African continent?:
    a) Cape Town - Pretoria   b) Algiers – Conakry
    c) Cairo - Dar-e-Salaam   d) Angola - Zimbabwe

8. The Great Trunk Route passes through
    a) Mediterranean Sea - Indian Ocean
    b) North Atlantic Ocean
    c) South Atlantic Ocean
    d) North Pacific Ocean

9. The transcontinental Stuart Highway passes through-
    a) Darwin and Melbourne   b) Edmonton and Anchorage
    c) Vancouver and St. John's City   d) Chengdu and Lhasa

10. What is the correct order of launching the following satellites?
    A - ARYABHATTA,   B - ROHINI,   C - BHASKAR
    a) A, B, C   b) A, C, B   c) B, C, A   d) C, B, A

11. Criss-cross highways connecting major cities in which country?
    a) China   b) USA
    b) India   d) Russia

Answers: 1-b, 2-a, 3-c, 4-c, 5-c, 6-a, 7-a, 8-b, 9-a, 10-b, 11-a,

CHAPTER 8 - INTERNATIONAL TRADE

1. **What is international trade? Give its importance in modern economies.**
   a) International trade refers to the exchange of goods and services among countries across national boundaries.
   b) International trade bridges the gap between surplus regions and deficit regions through export and imports.
   c) Countries need to trade to obtain commodities, they cannot produce themselves or they can purchase elsewhere at a lower price.
   d) It helps countries in maintaining the specialization in the production of goods and services.
   e) It increases international cooperation and understanding.
   f) In early times it played significant role in the cultural diffusion.

2. **What is Barter System, the initial form of trade?**
   a) Primitive societies practised the barter system for trade where direct exchange of goods took place.
   b) In this system needs were exchanged with services or things.
   c) Before paper and coin currency came into being, rare objects with very high intrinsic value served as money.
   d) The difficulties of barter system were overcome by the introduction of money.
   e) **Jon Beel Mela** takes place in Jagiroad near Guwahati, it is possibly the only fair In India, where barter system is still alive.

3. **Describe the changes that have occurred in international trade since ancient times to present century.**
   a) In ancient times, trade was restricted to local markets because transporting goods over long distances was risky.
   b) Trading commodities were of basic necessity – food and clothes. Only the rich people bought jewellery, costly dresses and this resulted in trade of luxury items.
   c) During Roman Empire, trade was done through the Silk Route from Rome to China (6,000 km route).

d) European traded goods through ocean ships in 12/13th century.

e) 15th century onwards, a new form of trade emerged which was called **slave trade.** African natives were captured and forcefully transported to the newly discovered regions for their labour in the plantations.

f) After the Industrial Revolution, the industrialised nations imported raw materials and exported the value added finished products back to the non-industrialised nations.

g) In the later half of the 19th century, industrial nations traded finished goods between themselves each other's principle customers.

h) During the postwar period, organisations like the World Trade Organisation helped in promoting international trade.

4. Describe the basis of international trade.

The basis of international trade is:

A. **Difference in national resources:** Trade arises because of regional differences in production and productivity. It also arises because of great variations in the location and distribution of natural resources. Trade arises when the production of certain goods and services exceeds the local consumption levels and it is in short supply elsewhere.

B. **Population:** Country having large size of population cannot trade goods outside the country due to high local demand.

C. **Stage of economic development**: In agriculturally important countries, agro products are exchanged for manufactured goods whereas industrialised nations export machinery and finished products and import food grains and other raw materials.

D. **Extent of foreign investment**: Foreign investment can boost trade in developing countries which lack in capital required for the development of industries and agriculture.

E. **Transport**: With expansions of rail, ocean and air transport, better means of refrigeration and preservation, trade has expanded.

5. What is balance of trade?

a) Trade balance is the amount of import-export done by a country with other countries.

b) If the amount of import is more then the trade balance will be negative and if the amount of export is more then the trade balance will be positive.

c) Trade balance has serious implications for the economy of a country. Negative balance means that the country spends more on purchasing goods than it earns from selling, hence negative trade balance is not considered good for any country.

6. What are the two Types of international trade? Explain characteristics of each.

The two type of international trade are:

A. Bilateral trade-

a) In this type of trade the exchange of commodities is between two countries.

b) If the two countries are complementary to each other the bilateral trade will occur.

c) It occurs when one country exports raw material and energy sources to the other in exchange of manufacturing goods.

B. Multilateral trade-

a) In this type of trade the commodities are exchanged between many countries.

b) The countries may not be complementary to each other.

c) The direction of trade is diversified which means that each country export a number of goods.

7. What is free trade? Explain its effects on economies of developing countries.

a) Free trade is the act of opening up economies for trading. This is done by bringing down trade barriers like tariffs.

b) Free trade allows goods and services from everywhere to compete with domestic products and services.

c) It can adversely affect the economies by not giving equal playing field.

d) Foreign products which are cheaper can destroy local production and thus may create unemployment.

e) Imposing conditions which are unfavourable.

f) **Dumped goods** of cheaper prices can harm the domestic producers.

8. What are the basic functions of the World Trade Organization (WTO)?

a) It was formed in 1948 as GATT (General Agreement for Tariffs and Trade) and from January 1995 it was converted into WTO (World Trade Organization).

b) Its main objective is to make efforts to get rid of high customs duty and various other types of barriers.

c) WTO sets the rules of global trade.

d) It also settles disputes between its member countries.

e) It provides services like telecommunication, banking etc.

f) It also includes trade of intellectual property rights in its functions.

g) Its headquarters is located in Geneva and it has 164 member countries.

h) India is its founding member country.

9. What are Regional trading blocs? State its objectives.

1. Trading blocs is the groups of countries which have formal systems of trading agreements.

2. Most of the international trade has been taking place within these blocs.

   Objectives And Importace of Trading Blocs

a) Its main objective is to reduce tariffs and quotas on imports between the member countries.

b) It regulates the trade within the bloc and with other trading blocs of the world.

c) To encourage free trade between member countries.

d) It helps in increasing economic relations among member's countries.

e) Geographical distance between the member countries and historical and cultural relationships.

f) Geo-political reasons such as controlling trade in a particular commodity and retaining the power.

g) Similarities and complementarities in trading items.

10. Describe the concerns related to international trade.

a) International trade has many advantages but it can be damaging/harmful.

b) It leads to more and more dependence on other countries.

c) It creates uneven levels of development between countries and regions.

d) It leads to exploitation and commercial rivalry between nations and which in turn leads to wars.

e) It affects the environment, health and well being of people.

11. Explain how the global trade affects many aspects of life.

a) Global trade affects the environment, health and well-being of the people.

b) Due to competition between countries to trade more, production and the use of natural resources has increased.

c) Resources are used faster than they can renew themselves. As a result, marine life and forests are depleting fast.

d) Multinational corporations trading in oil, gas mining, pharmaceuticals and agri-business are exploiting local resources and creating more pollution.

e) Health and well being of people is affected due to pollution and depletion of resources.

12. Why sea ports and harbours are also known as 'Gateways of International Trade?

1. Sea port is a place on sea coast where cargo is received from other countries as imports and sent out as exports.

2. Port has facilities for loading and unloading cargo.

Sea ports and harbours are the important gateways of international trade because-

a) It acts as a point of exit and entry for a country.

b) Cargoes and travellers pass from one part of the world to another through these ports.

c) These ports provide facilities of docking, loading, unloading and the storage facilities for cargo.

d) The quantity of cargo handled by a port is an indicator of the level of development.

13. What are the different types of ports?

1. Types of port according to cargo handled-

a) **Industrial Ports**: These ports specialise in bulk cargo-like grain, sugar, ore, oil, chemicals and similar materials.

b) **Commercial Ports**: These ports handle general cargo-packaged products and manufactured good. These ports also handle passenger traffic.

c) **Comprehensive Ports**: Such ports handle bulk and general cargo in large volumes.

2. Types of ports classified on the basis of their location.

a) **Inland port**: These ports are located away from the sea coast. They are linked with the sea by river or a canal. Such ports are suitable for only flat bottom ships. **Kolkata** is located on river Hugli, **Manchester**.

b) **Out ports**: These are deep water ports built away from the actual port. These act as a parent port. They receive ships which are large in size and thus are unable to dock at the actual port. **Athens and Piraeus in Greece.**

3. Types of ports on the basis of the specialized tasks:

a) **Oil ports**: These ports deals in processing and shipping of oil. Some of these are tanker and some refinery ports. E.g.**Tripoli**

b) **Naval ports**: These ports are of strategic importance. They serve only warships. E.g. **Kochi**.

c) **Entrepot ports**: These ports act as a collection centres. Imported goods are collected and shipped to different countries as exports. E.g. **Singapore**.

d) **Packet stations**: they are also known as ferry ports. They are concerned with passengers and mail across water bodies covering short distances. They occur in pairs across water body. E.g. **Dover and Calais**.

e) **Ports of call**: These ports provide facilities such as refueling, watering, taking food items to ships on route to other countries. E.g. **Aden**

Objectives

1. Where is the headquarter of World Trade Organisation located?
   a) Vienna
   b) Geneva
   c) Minsk
   d) Jakarta

2. Which one is not an example of an entrepot port?
   a) Singapore
   b) Rotterdam
   c) Copenhagen
   d) Honolulu

3. Most of the great ports of the world are classified as:
   a) Naval Ports
   b) Comprehensive Ports
   c) Oil Ports
   d) Industrial Ports

4. What is the full form of MFN?
   a) Major Favoured Nation
   b) Major Fulfilled Network
   c) Most Favoured Network
   d) Most Favoured Nation

5. Which one of the following statements is not correct?
   a) Trade is a voluntary exchange of goods and services.
   b) There must be a party to trade.
   c) Trade is beneficial to both the parties.
   d) Barter is a form of trade.

6. John Beale Fair, where the barter system is still alive. This fair is held near which city?
   a) Kolkata
   b) Dehradun
   c) Guwahati
   d) Tuticorin

7. How many countries are members of WTO-
   a) 135
   b) 118
   c) 155
   d) 164

8. Which of the following pairs is correctly matched?

Country	Oil Port
a) Tunisia	Tripoli
b) Lebanon	Eskhira
c) Venezuela	Maracaibo
d) Oman	Aden

9. Which one is not a basis of International Trade?

(a) Polulation size   (b) Area of the country

(c) Foreign investment   (d) Transport

10. The Silk Route connected:

a) India – Persia   b) China – Persia

c) China – Rome   d) India – China

11. Which one is not a positive aspect of international trade?

a) Better standard of living   b) Equalisation of prices and wages

c) Commercial rivalry   d) Diffusion of knowledge/culture

12. When was GATT transformed into World Trade Organisation?

a) 1 January 1994   b) 1 July 1994

c) 1 January 1995   d) 1 July 1995

13. How much trade generated by regional blocs in the world trade.

a) 30%   b) 52%

c) 65%   d) 72%

14. Which country was the first to abolish the slave trade?

a) Great Bratain   b) Spain

c) Denmark   d) United States

15. When countries imposed trade taxes for the first time?

a) During the World Wars   b) After the Industrial Revolution

c) After the Roman Empire   d) In the nineteenth century

Answers: 1-b, 2-d, 3-b, 4-d, 5-b, 6-c, 7-d, 8-c, 9-b, 10-c, 11-c, 12-c, 13-b, 14-c, 15-a

BOOK 2 – INDIA PEOPLE AND ECONOMY

CHAPTER 1 - POPULATION DISTRIBUTION, DENSITY, GROWTH AND COMPOSITION

1. What is population? What are the sources of population data in India?

I. The number of people living in a particular area in a given time period is called population.

II. India is the second most populous country after China in the world with its total population of 1,210 million (2011).

III. India's population is larger than the total population of North & South America and Australia put together.

The following are the sources of population data in India-

a) By collecting data through census every 10 years, the first census was conducted in 1872 and the first complete census was conducted in 1881.

b) By civil register registration

c) By sample survey

2. Explain the highly uneven distribution of population in India.

a) Population distribution in India is highly uneven.

b) Top 10 states like Uttar Pradesh, Maharashtra, Bihar, West Bengal, Tamil Nadu, Madhya Pradesh, Rajasthan, Karnataka, Gujarat and Andhra Pradesh account for 76% of the total population of the country.

c) States like Jammu and Kashmir, Arunachal Pradesh and Uttarakhand have small population size despite their large geographical area.

d) Rajasthan due to development of irrigation, Jharkhand due to availability of mineral and energy resources and peninsular states due to development of transport network have become areas of medium to high population.

e) It is a close relationship between population and physical socio-economic and historical factors for uneven distribution of population in India.

3. **Explain with examples the factors which determines the pattern of the population distribution in India.**

   Uneven distribution of population in India suggests a close relationship between population and physical, socioeconomic and historical factors.

   A. **Physical factors** such as Climate, Terrain and Availability of water influenced and determined the pattern of the population distribution.

   Example 1: the North Indian Plains, deltas and Coastal Plains have higher proportion of population because they have climate suitable for agriculture and fertile soil.

   Example 2: Mountainous and forested regions of southern and central Indian States, Himalayan states, and some of the north-eastern states are less populated.

   Example 3: Development of irrigation (Rajasthan), availability of mineral and energy resources (Jharkhand) and development of transport network (Peninsular States) have resulted in moderate to high proportion of population.

   B. **Socio-economic and historical factors** :

   Example 1: Traditional settled agriculture and early human settlement has resulted in large population in the river plains and coastal areas of India.

   Example 2: Development of transport and better agricultural development has resulted in large population in North Plains.

   C. **The industrialization and urbanization** also influenced the distribution of population.

   Example 1: The urban regions of Delhi, Mumbai, Kolkata, Bangalore, etc. have high concentration of population due to industrial development and urbanization. A large numbers of rural-urban migrants come to these towns.

   D. **Religious and linguistic factor**: People moving out of their native places tend to settle in those areas where there are people with language, culture, food habits that are like theirs. It is common to find cities having residential areas which are communal in nature.

4. **What do you mean by Density of population?**

   It is defined as the number of persons per unit area. It helps in getting a better understanding of the spatial distribution of population in relation to land.

5. **What do you mean by physiological or agricultural densities?**

   It is expressed as number of persons per cultivable land. It helps in getting better understanding of pressure of population on total cultivable land.

   $$\textbf{Physiological density} = \frac{\text{Total population}}{\text{Net cultivated area}}$$

   $$\textbf{Agricultural density} = \frac{\text{Total agricultural population}}{\text{Net cultivable area}}$$

6. **Describe the spatial variations of population densities in our country.**

   (a) Density of population ranges from as low as 17 persons per sq km in Arunachal Pradesh to 11297 persons in the National Capital Territory of Delhi.

   (b) Among the Indian States, Bihar (1102), West Bengal (1029), Kerala (859) and Uttar Pradesh (828) have higher densities.

   (c) States like Haryana (573), Tamilnadu (555), Punjab (550) and Jharkhand (414) have moderate densities.

   (d) The hill states of the Himalayan region and North eastern states of India (excluding Assam) have relatively low densities.

   (e) After Delhi, the Union Territories of Chandigarh (9252), Daman-Diu and Dadra & Nagar Haveli (2867), Puducherry (2598) and Lakshadweep (2013) have high population density.

   (f) After the Arunachal Pradesh (17), the lowest population density is found in Mizoram (52), Sikkim (86) and Nagaland (119), while among union territories, the lowest population density is found in Andaman and Nicobar Islands (46).

7. **Define the term Growth of population. What are the two components of Population growth?**

Growth of population is the change in the number of people living in a particular area between two points of time. Its rate is expressed in percentage. It can be +ve or –ve.

It has two components namely;

A. **Natural growth**: it occurs due to change in birth and death rates.

B. **Induced Growth**: it is occurs due to change in immigration and emigration.

8. **Explain four distinct phases of growth of India's population.**

Phase I:

a) The period from 1901-1921 is referred to as a period of stagnant or stationary phase of growth of India's population.

b) In this period growth rate was very low, even recording a negative growth rate during 1911-1921.

c) Both the birth and death rate were high keeping the rate of increase low.

d) Poor health and medical services, illiteracy of people at large and inefficient distribution system of food and other basic necessities were largely responsible for a high birth and death rates in this period.

Phase II:

a) The decades 1921-1951 are referred to as the period of steady population growth.

b) An overall improvement in health and sanitation throughout the country brought down the mortality rate.

c) At the same time better transport and communication system improved distribution system.

d) The crude birth rate remained high in this period leading to higher growth rate than the previous phase.

Phase III:

a) The decades 1951-1981 are referred to as the period of population explosion in India.

b) It caused by a rapid fall in death rate but a high birth rate.

c) The average annual growth rate was as high as 2.2 per cent.

d) High birth rate was due to developmental activities and growing economy which improved people's living condition.

e) Beside it, due to increased international immigration from Tibet, Bangladesh, Nepal and Pakistan growth rate was high.

Phase IV:

a) After 1981 till present, the growth rate has started slowing down gradually.

b) It is due to decline in crude birth rate.

c) It is also due to an increase in the mean age at marriage, improved quality of life particularly education of females in the country.

9. **Describe the wide regional variation in growth rates of population from one state to another in India.**

i. Southern states Kerala, Karnataka, Tamil Nadu, Andhra Pradesh, Orissa, Pondicherry, and Goa have low growth rates (less than 20%), with Kerala registering the lowest growth rate (9.4).

ii. A continuous belt of states from west to east in the northern and central parts of the country have higher population growth rates than the southern states. States in this belt like Gujarat, Maharashtra, Punjab, Sikkim, Haryana, Uttar Pradesh, etc. have an average growth rate of 20-25%.

iii. During 2001-11, the population growth rate in all states and union territories has been slower than in the previous decade.

10. **"If the adolescent population is not guided properly, they can be quite vulnerable." Explain the statement.**

a) The adolescent population is considered to be the age group of 10-19 years which is 20.9% of the total population.

b) The adolescent population comprises 52.7% boys and 47.3% girls.

c) Early marriage, illiteracy – especially female illiteracy, tendency to drop out of school are the main problems faced by the adolescent population.

d) Due to low intake of nutrients, there is a risk of increased maternal mortality rate, physical and mental disability or retardation etc. of adolescent mothers.

e) Lack of employment opportunities increases the use of alcohol and drugs and juvenile crimes.

f) Thus, if the adolescent population is not nurtured and guided properly, then this age group will not be able to use its energy properly in nation building.

11. What is the main objective of "Beti Bachao Beti Padhao" social campaign?

a) Beti Bachao Beti Padhao (BBBP) scheme was launched on 22 January 2015 by the Prime Minister of India.

b) Beti Bachao Beti Padhao is being run by the Ministry of Women and Child Development, Health and Family Welfare and Human Resource Development.

c) Beti Bachao Beti Padhao is launched with the aim to address the falling Child Sex Ratio (CSR) and other issues related to women empowerment.

d) To help eliminate gender-based discrimination and discrimination.

e) For the safety and protection of girl child.

f) To provide education to girl child and enable their participation.

12. Describe the features of National Youth Policy 2014 for the overall development of youth and adolescent population.

a) National Youth Policy was launched in 2003 which was revised in the year 2014.

b) According to National Youth Policy 2014, the age group of 15-29 is defined as 'youth'.

c) It emphasizes on the all-round improvement of youth and adolescents.

d) It enables them to take responsibility for the constructive development of the country.

e) Its objective is to develop and strengthen the qualities of patriotism and responsible citizen.

f) Special emphasis was laid on empowering women and girls to bring equality in the status of men and women.

g) Efforts were made to promote new innovations, sports and entertainment, creativity and awareness in the field of science and technology.

13. What are the main objectives of "Skill Development and Entrepreneurship Policy"?

a) The Government of India has made a policy for skill development and entrepreneurship in 2015.

b) Its main objective is to provide a framework for skill related activities happening across the country.

c) To bind all activities with a standard.

d) To link various skills with the center

14. Define population composition.

Population composition is a separate field of study under population geography. In this, the following characteristics of the population are studied-

a) Analysis of age and sex

b) Study of rural-urban characteristics on the basis of place of residence

c) Study of ethnic and tribal characteristics

d) Study of language, religion, marital status

e) Analysis of literacy and education

f) Analysis of occupational characteristics of the population

15. Describe the uneven distribution of rural population in India.

a) 68.8% of the total population of the country lives in rural areas.

b) States like Bihar and Sikkim have a very high percentage of rural population, while the states of Goa and Maharashtra have a low percentage of rural population.

c) The proportion of rural population in Dadra and Nagar Haveli is 53.38%.

d) The size of villages is also less than 200 persons in the North Eastern states, Western Rajasthan and Rann of Kutch in Gujarat and the size of villages in the states of Kerala and Maharashtra is found to be up to 17 thousand persons.

e) The extent of rural-urban migration at inter-state and intra-state level controls the concentration of rural population.
   in degree of urbanization and extent of rural-urban migration.

16. Describe the uneven distribution of urban population in India.

a) There is wide variation across the country in the distribution of urban population.

b) The level of urbanisation is higher in areas which are well connected by main road and rail links etc., such as the North Indian plains.

c) There is high rural-urban migration in the industrial areas around Delhi, Mumbai, Kolkata, Chennai etc., hence these cities have large urban population.

d) The urban population is low in the middle and lower Gangetic plains and also in the non-irrigated western Rajasthan and the remote hilly tribal areas of the North East.

e) The urban population is low in the flood prone areas of the peninsular states and the level of urbanisation is low in the agriculturally less developed middle and lower Gangetic plains and the eastern part of Madhya Pradesh.

17. Mention the features of linguistic organization in India.

a) India is a country with a huge linguistic diversity.

b) According to the linguistic survey (1903-28, by Grierson), there were 179 languages and about 544 dialects in the country.

c) 22 languages have been scheduled in the constitution of modern India- Assamese, Bengali, Bodo, Dogri, Gujarati, Hindi, Kannada, Kashmiri, Konkani, Maithili, Malayalam, Manipuri,

Marathi, Nepali, Oriya, Punjabi, Sanskrit, Santhali, Sindhi, Tamil, Telugu and Urdu are the 22 official languages of the country.

d) Among the scheduled languages, Hindi is the largest and Sanskrit, Bodo and Manipuri are the smallest language groups.

e) The boundaries of linguistic regions in the country are not definite and clear but are superimposed on their respective border regions.

18. Name the four language families in India.

The languages spoken in India are divided into the four language families-

A. **Indo-European (Aryan)**- 73% of the population uses this language family, Indo-European (Aryan) is the most widely spoken language among the four language families. Iranian (Persian) branch of Indo-Aryan language is spoken outside India. Dardic language branch is spoken in Jammu and Kashmir. Indo-Aryan language branch is spoken in Uttar Pradesh, Rajasthan, Haryana, Madhya Pradesh, Bihar, Gujarat, Maharashtra and Goa.

B. **Dravidian (Dravidian)**- 20% of the population uses this language family. South Dravidian, Central Dravidian and North Dravidian are its major language groups. South Dravidian branch is spoken in Tamil Nadu, Karnataka and Kerala. Central Dravidian branch is spoken in Andhra Pradesh, Telangana, Orissa, MP and Maharashtra. North Dravidian branch is spoken in Bihar, West Bengal, West Bengal, and West Bengal. Spoken in Bengal, Jharkhand etc.

C. **Austric (Nishad)**- 1.38% of the population uses this language family, Austro-Asiatic and Austro-Nesian (outside India) are its sub-language families. Mon Khmer (Meghalaya, Nicobar Islands) and Munda language (West Bengal, Bihar, Jharkhand, Orissa, Madhya Pradesh and Maharashtra) are the major branches of this family.

D. **Sino-Tibetan (Kirat)**- Only 0.85% of the population uses this language family. Tibeto-Myanmar sub-family is spoken in

Tibeto-Himalayan region (J. & K., Himachal Pradesh, Sikkim etc. Siamese-Chinese language sub-family is spoken in Assam, Nagaland, Manipur, Mizoram, Tripura and Meghalaya states under Assam-Myanmar branch.

19. **Describe the religious composition of the population of India.**

    Religion is the major force influencing cultural and political life. Religion virtually pervades almost all aspects of the family and community life of the people. The spatial distribution of religious communities in the country can be seen as follows-

    a) **Hindu community**- Hindu population is 79.8% of the total population of the country, they are the major religious community in many states like Haryana, Himachal Pradesh, UP, Bihar etc. Their concentration is less in the states of Sikkim, Punjab, Jammu and Kashmir and Mizoram.

    b) **Muslim community**- Muslims are the largest religious minority community in India. They are in majority in Jammu and Kashmir, West Bengal and Kerala, some districts of Uttar Pradesh and Delhi and Lakshadweep.

    c) **Christian community**- This community is mostly distributed in the rural areas of the country. The main concentration is seen along the western coast around Goa and Kerala and in the hills of Meghalaya, Mizoram, Nagaland and Manipur.

    d) **Sikh community**- This community is mostly concentrated in a relatively small area of the country, particularly in the states of Punjab, Haryana and Delhi.

    e) **Jains and Buddhists**- Jains and Buddhists are the smallest religious groups in India. Jains are concentrated in urban areas of Rajasthan, Gujarat and Maharashtra. Buddhists are mostly concentrated in Maharashtra, Sikkim, Arunachal Pradesh and Ladakh, Lahul and Spiti in Himachal, etc.

    f) **Others**- Other religions in India include Zoroastrian, tribal and other indigenous religions and beliefs. These groups are concentrated in small clusters throughout the country.

20. **How do the formal expressions of religions appear on the landscape?**

Religion is a major force influencing cultural and political life. Religion pervades almost all aspects of people's family and community life. Religion affects the landscape in the following ways:

a) The design of religious places and buildings, the use of cemeteries, etc. vary according to religion.

b) Plants, animals and trees have different significance for different religions.

c) There is variation in the size, type, location, use and number of places of worship.

21. **What is the difference between main worker and marginal worker as per the standard census definition?**

A. **Main worker** – A person who works for at least 183 days or 6 months in a year is called a main worker.

B. **Marginal worker** – A person who works for less than 183 days in a year is called a marginal worker.

22. **Describe the variations in the working population ratio in India.**

a) The age group of 15-59 is known as the working population segment, which has spatial variation within the country.

b) Goa has a low proportion of working population while Mizoram has a high proportion of working population.

c) States with a large percentage of workers are Himachal Pradesh, Sikkim, Chhattisgarh, Andhra Pradesh, Karnataka, Arunachal Pradesh, Nagaland, Manipur and Meghalaya.

d) Among the Union Territories, Dadra and Nagar Haveli and Daman and Diu have high participation rate.

e) Work participation rate is higher in regions with lower level of economic development, this is because large number of manual workers are required to carry out subsistence or near subsistence economic activities.

23. Describe the occupational structure of the population of India.

a) The occupational structure of the population of India shows a larger proportion of primary sector workers than the secondary and tertiary sectors.

b) About 54.6% of the total working population are cultivators and agricultural labourers. Only 3.8% workers are engaged in household industries. 41.6% are engaged in trade and commerce, construction and repairs etc.

c) The number of male workers is relatively higher than the number of female workers in all sectors.

d) The proportion of workers in the agricultural sector was found to be 54.6% in 2011, 3.8% in the secondary sector and 41.6% in the tertiary sector.

e) The highest participation of female labour is about 37.09% in the primary sector.

24. What is labour participation rate? Describe the variations in work participation rate across different sectors of India's economy.

The ratio of working population to the total population is called labour participation rate. This rate varies from one region to another.

a) States like Himachal Pradesh and Nagaland have a very high number of farmers.

b) On the other hand, states like Andhra Pradesh, Chhattisgarh, Orissa, Jharkhand, West Bengal and Madhya Pradesh have a high proportion of agricultural labourers.

c) Highly urbanised areas like Delhi, Chandigarh and Pondicherry have a very large proportion of workers engaged in other services.

d) This indicates not only the availability of limited cultivable land but also the need for more workers in non-agricultural sectors brought about by large-scale urbanisation and industrialisation.

25. Explain the sectoral shift in the country's economy.

a) The ratio of workers in the agricultural sector has shown a decline over the last few decades from 58.2% in 2001 to 54.6% (2011). ii) As a result, the participation rate in the secondary and tertiary sectors has increased.

b) The main reason for this is the increased dependence of workers from farm-based employment to non-farm based employment.

c) This is called sectoral transfer in the country's economy.

<u>Objectives</u>

1. Consider the following statements and choose the incorrect option from the given options:
   a)   India has a population greater than the population of North America, South America and Australia put together.
   b)   The first complete census of India was conducted in 1872.
   c)   India has second largest populated country in the world.
   d)   Census operation held every 10 years in our country.

2. Which of the following is not correctly matched?
   a) Highest population – Uttar Pradesh
   b) Lowest population – Sikkim
   c) Highest density – West Bengal
   d) Lowest density – Arunachal Pradesh

3. Which decade has negative decadal growth?
   a) 1901-11   b) 1911-21
   c) 1921-31   d) 1941-51

4. Which decade had the highest decadal growth?
   a) 2001-11   b) 1991-2001
   c) 1981-91   d) 1961-71

5. In which year was the Skill Development and Entrepreneurship Policy launched?
   a) 2014   b) 2015
   c) 2016   d) 2017

6. Which one of the following is the largest linguistic group in India?
   a) Sino-Tibetan
   b) Austric
   c) Indo-Aryan
   d) Dravidian

7. Who are called marginal workers?
   a) Those who work less than 183 days in a year.
   b) Those who work more than 183 days in a year.
   c) Those who are unemployed workers.
   d) Those who are engaged in the agricultural sector.

8. Read the given statements and choose the correct statement/statements-
   I. There are 544 languages and 179 dialects in the country.
   II. 22 languages have been scheduled in the 8th Schedule of the Constitution.
   III. Sanskrit, Bodo, Manipuri are the smallest language group.
   IV. The largest language family is the Dravidian language family.
   a) I, II, III and IV
   b) I, II and III
   c) III and IV
   d) II and III

9. What is the national sex ratio of 0-6 age group?
   a) 927
   b) 933
   c) 945
   d) 895

10. Which group of states is arranged in the correct assending order of population density?
    a) Arunachal Pradesh, Sikkim, Nagaland, Mizoram
    b) Arunachal Pradesh, Mizoram, Nagaland, Sikkim
    c) Arunachal Pradesh, Mizoram, Sikkim, Nagaland
    d) Arunachal Pradesh, Nagaland, Mizoram, Sikkim

11. Which language group is not scheduled in the Constitution?
    a) Maithi – Bodo
    b) Santhali – Dogri
    b) Nepali – Sindhi
    d) Rajasthani - English

Answers: 1-b, 2-c, 3-b, 4-d, 5-b, 6-c, 7-a, 8-d, 9-a, 10-c, 11-d

CHAPTER 2 - HUMAN SETTLEMENT

1. **Define human settlement. What is the basis of classification of settlements?**

   Human settlement means any type or size of dwelling where humans live.

   a) Settlements are differentiated on the basis of urban and rural, population can be a parameter for this.

   b) Differentiation on the basis of functions performed by the population is more important.

   c) Rural settlement is involved in primary activities and urban settlement is involved in secondary and tertiary activities.

   d) Settlements can also be classified on the basis of their shape and pattern, such as dense and sparse settlement.

2. **Explain the basic difference between rural and urban settlements.**

   The basic differences between rural and urban settlements are as follows:

   a) Rural settlements derive their life support or basic economic needs from land-based primary economic activities, whereas, urban settlements, depend on processing of raw materials on one hand and manufacturing of various kinds of services on the other.

   b) Cities act as nodes of economic development. Urban settlements provide goods and services to the people of rural settlements and in return rural settlements provide food and raw materials. This functional relationship between urban and rural settlements takes place through transport and communication networks.

   c) Rural people are less mobile and, therefore, social relations between them are intimate. The way of life in urban areas is complex and fast-paced, and social relations are formal.

   d) Rural settlements are small in size as they depend on extensive lands for cultivation etc. whereas urban settlements are large and dense.

3. **Major factors determining rural settlement.**

   Residents of rural settlement are engaged in primary activities and the size of the settlement is small. The factors influencing rural settlement are as follows-

   a) Easy access to water supply, river bank or lake
   b) Fertile land and soil area
   c) High land to avoid flood, insects etc.
   d) Easy availability of house building material wood, stone etc.
   e) Small or high place to avoid war, disturbance etc.

4. **Explain three factors and conditions responsible for different types of rural settlements in India.**

   The types of settlement are determined by the extent of built-up area and inter-house distance. The three factors are:

   A. Physical factors –

   a) Nature of terrain: - Dispersed type of settlements are found in remote forests, small hills of Himachal Pradesh. Compact settlements are found in the highly productive alluvial plains of Punjab.
   b) Altitude: - Dislocated settlements are found in the hills of Meghalaya and clustered and semi-clustered settlements are found in the plains of Gujarat.
   c) Climate: - Settlement may be disrupted due to frequent droughts.
   d) Availability of water: - Compact settlements have developed in Rajasthan due to scarcity of water.

   B. Cultural and ethnic factors-

   a) Caste and tribe structure: - Due to ethnic factors the settlement may be fragmented and hamlets like Chhattisgarh.
   b) Religion - People of the same religion prefer to live together forming a basti or larger one.
   C. **Security factors –** Due to protection from dacoits, wild animals or fear settlements may form clustered and compact settlements.

5. Describe the four types of rural settlements found in India

The type of rural settlement in India is determined by the extent of built-up area and inter-house distance. They are of 4 types:-

A. Clustered, Agglomerated and Nuclear Settlement:-

a) In this type of settlement the built up area is compact and the inter-house distance is small.

b) In this type of village the general living area is distinct and separated from the surrounding fields.

c) Such settlements are found in highly productive alluvial plains (Punjab), valleys of the Shivaliks (Dehradun) and in the North Eastern states.

d) Such settlements are also formed due to security and defence reasons (e.g. Madhya Pradesh) or for water or cultivable land (Rajasthan).

B. Semi-Clustered Settlements:-

a) In this type of settlement the built up area is less than that of the agglomerated settlement.

b) It may result from the isolation or fragmentation of a large compact village.

c) Some sections of the village society choose or are forced to live a little away from the main cluster or village.

d) The land-owners and dominant communities live in the central part of the main village, while people of lower status of settlement live in the outskirts of the village.

e) Such settlements are found in the plains of Gujarat and some parts of Rajasthan.

C. Hamleted Settlement:-

a) When a large settlement gets divided into many small units physically separated from each other but having a common name, it takes the form of a basti.

b) This is due to social and ethnic factors.

c) These small units of settlements are known as panna, para, palli, nagla, dhani etc.

d) Such settlements are found in the plains of Ganga, lower valleys of Himalayas.

D. Dispersed Settlement:-

a) When a settlement consists of a few isolated huts it is called a dispersed settlement.

b) This type of settlements is found in remote forests, small hills with few hillocks and pastures on the slopes.

c) This results in extremely fragmented and little resource support.

d) These are found in Meghalaya, Uttaranchal, Himachal Pradesh and Kerala.

6. What are urban settlements?

a) Urban settlements are generally dense and large in size.

b) They are engaged in various non-economic, economic and administrative functions.

c) They are functionally linked with the rural areas surrounding them.

d) Thus, they are directly linked with the villages and also with each other.

7. Urbanization in India

a) Urbanization is measured as the percentage of urban population to the total population.

b) The level of urbanization in India in 2011 was 31.16%, which is much lower than developed countries.

c) The urban population has increased 11 times in the 20th century.

d) The growth of urban centers and the emergence of new cities have led to an increase in urban population and urbanization.

e) The highest growth of urban population occurred in the decade 1971-81.

f) The growth rate of urbanization has slowed down in the last 2 decades.

g) Goa is the state with the highest and Himachal Pradesh with the lowest urbanization.

8. Standards for urban settlement in India

a) The population density should be 400 persons per square km.

b) There should be a Municipal Corporation, Municipality, Nagar Panchayat or Cantonment.

c) More than 75% of the male population should be engaged in non-primary activities.

d) Population size should be more than 5000 persons.

9. Describe the classification of Indian cities on the basis of their development in different periods.

Towns in India flourished since prehistoric times. On the basis of their development in different periods, Indian cities can be classified as:

A. Ancient Towns :-

a) Towns with long history of existence and which are more than 2000 years old are called ancient cities.

b) These cities developed as religious and cultural centres.

c) Important cities are - Varanasi, Ayodhya, Prayag, Pataliputra, Madurai, etc.

B. Medieval Cities :-

a) Towns which emerged during medieval period as headquarters of states are called medieval towns.

b) Important cities are - Delhi, Hyderabad, Jaipur, Lucknow, Agra, etc.

C. Modern Cities :-

a) Pre-independence towns : These towns were developed by British and other European rulers. They were port cities such as Mumbai, Kolkata, Chennai, Surat, Goa and Pondicherry. Later some hill stations and summer resorts were developed from them such as Shimla, etc.

b) Cities after Independence:- These cities were developed as administrative centres such as Chandigarh, Bhubaneswar, Gandhinagar.

c) Some developed as industrial cities such as Jamshedpur, Durgapur, Bhilai, Sindri, Barauni.

d) Some old cities were also developed as satellite cities around metropolitan cities such as Ghaziabad, Rohtak, Gurgaon around Delhi.

10. **Functional Classification of Cities.**

On the basis of main or specialized functions Indian cities are broadly classified in the following manner-

A. **Administrative Towns**- Cities with administrative headquarters of higher order are called administrative towns. Such as Chandigarh, New Delhi, Bhopal, Shillong, Guwahati, Imphal, Srinagar, Gandhinagar, Jaipur, Chennai etc.

B. **Industrial Towns**- The main driving force behind the development of Mumbai, Salem, Coimbatore, Modinagar, Jamshedpur, Hooghly, Bhilai, etc. has been the development of industries.

C. **Transport Towns**- These may be port towns which are mainly engaged in import and export activities, e.g. Kandla, Kochi, Kozhikode, Visakhapatnam, etc. or hubs of internal transport e.g. Dhule, Mughalsarai, Itarsi, Katni, etc.

D. **Commercial Towns**- Cities and towns specialised in trade and commerce are placed in this category. Kolkata, Saharanpur, Satna, etc. are some examples.

E. **Mining Towns**- These towns have developed in mineral rich areas e.g. Raniganj, Jharia, Digboi, Ankleshwar, Singrauli, etc.

F. **Garrison Towns**- These towns have emerged as garrison towns e.g. Ambala, Jalandhar, Mhow, Babina, Udhampur, etc.

G. **Religious and cultural towns**- Varanasi, Mathura, Amritsar, Madurai, Puri, Ajmer, Pushkar, Tirupati, Kurukshetra, Haridwar, Ujjain became famous due to their religious importance.

H. **Educational towns**- Some of the main campus towns developed as educational centres like Roorkee, Varanasi, Aligarh, Pilani, Allahabad.

I. **Tourist towns**- Nainital, Mussoorie, Shimla, Pachmarhi, Jodhpur, Jaisalmer, Udagamandalam, Ooty, Mount Abu are some tourist destinations.

11. What are the main objectives of Smart City Mission?

a) To promote cities to provide infrastructure, clean and sustainable environment and better life to the citizens.

b) To implement smart solutions for facilities and services.

c) To provide affordable facilities using less resources.

d) To develop an area that can act as a lighthouse for the growing city.

e) Focus is on sustainable and holistic development.

f) To develop as areas with low risk of natural disasters.

Objectives

1. According to the Census of India, which one of the following characteristics is not a part of the definition of a city?
   a) Population density 400 persons per sq. km.
   b) Presence of Municipality, Corporation
   c) More than 75% male population engaged in primary activities
   d) Population size more than 10000 persons

2. Which of the following cities is not an ancient city?
   a) Varanasi
   b) Delhi
   c) Patna
   d) Prayagraj

3. Which one of the following cities is not a medieval city?
   a) Madurai
   b) Hyderabad
   c) Jaipur
   d) Agra

4. Which one of the following is not a mining town?
   a) Kota
   b) Jharia
   c) Digboi
   d) Singrauli

5. What is urbanisation level in India according to Census 2011?
   a) 25.71%
   b) 27.78%
   c) 31.16%
   d) 35.08%

6. Which one of the following is a group of satellite cities?
   a) Ghaziabad, Gurugram
   b) Kandla, Kochi
   c) Mughalsarai, Itarsi
   d) Saharanpur, Satna

7. Which of the following is not a garrison town?

     a) Ambala
     b) Jalandhar
     c) Babina
     d) Darjeeling

8. Which one is not correctly matched-

     a) Nucleated   - Bundelkhand region of central India
     b) Fragmented   - Gujarat plain
     c) Hamleted   - Middle and lower Ganga plain
     d) Isolated.   - Lower valleys of the Himalayas

Read the following table and answer question no 09 to 11.

Year	Number of Towns/UAs	Urban Population (in Thousands)	% of Total Population	Decennial Growth (%)
1901	1,827	25,851.9	10.84	—
1911	1,815	25,941.6	10.29	0.35
1921	1,949	28,086.2	11.18	8.27
1931	2,072	33,456.0	11.99	19.12
1941	2,250	44,153.3	13.86	31.97
1951	2,843	62,443.7	17.29	41.42
1961	2,365	78,936.6	17.97	26.41
1971	2,590	1,09,114	19.91	38.23
1981	3,378	1,59,463	23.34	46.14
1991	4,689	2,17,611	25.71	36.47
2001	5,161	2,85.355	27.78	31.13
2011*	6,171	3,77,000	31.16	31.08

Source: Census of India, 2011 http.//www.censusindia.gov.in (Provisional)

9. In which decade did the maximum decadal growth of total urban population take place?

     a) 1961-71
     b) 1971-81
     c) 1981-91
     d) 1991-2001

10. How many towns increased in last decade of the given table?

     a) 5161
     b) 6171
     c) 1010
     d) 11332

11. How many population increased in last decade of the table?

     a) 285355
     b) 377000
     c) 662355
     d) 91645

Answers: 1-d, 2-b, 3-a, 4-a, 5-c, 6-a, 7-d, 8-d, 9-b, 10-c, 11-d

CHAPTER 3 - LAND RESOURSE AND AGRICULTURE

1. Explain three factors which influence the land use changes in a region.

   Three types of changes in an economy which affect land use are:

I. **The size of the economy:**
   a) With increase in the levels of income the pressure on land increases and marginal lands are brought under use.
   b) **For e.g.** With increase in industrial activities the agricultural lands are put under non-agricultural uses.

II. **Change in the composition of the economy**
   a) With growth in secondary and tertiary sector land use changes from agricultural uses to non-agricultural uses.
   b) **For e.g**. In Delhi city the agricultural land is being used for building purposes.

III. **Decline in agricultural sector**:
   a) The pressure on land for agricultural activities continues to be high because large number of people depends on agriculture and it feeds the large population.

2. **What is the difference between reporting area and geographical area?**
   a. In India, the land revenue department maintains land use records. The sum of land use categories is equal to the total reporting area, which is different from the geographical area.
   b. The Indian Survey Department is responsible for providing correct information about the geographical area of the administrative units of India.
   c. The basic difference between the land revenue and survey departments is that the area presented by the land revenue is based on the reporting area as per the papers, which may be less or more. The total geographical area is based on the survey of the Indian Survey Department and it is permanent.

3. Present the land use classification adopted by the land revenue records.

a. **Forest**- It is important to know that classified forest area and actual area under forests are different. The government has demarcated classified forest area in such a way that where forests can grow. This definition has been consistently adopted in land revenue records. Thus, an increase may be recorded in the area of this category but it does not mean that forests will actually be found there.

b. **Barren & Wasteland**- The land which cannot be made cultivable with the help of prevalent technology, such as barren hilly terrain, desert, ravines etc. have been classified as uncultivable wasteland.

c. **Land put to Non-agricultural uses**- This category includes land use for settlements (rural and urban), infrastructure (roads, canals etc.), industries, shops etc. The increase in secondary and tertiary activities leads to an increase in the land use of this category.

d. **Permanent pastures**: Most of this type of land is owned by the Gram Panchayat or the government. Only a small part of this land is in private ownership. The land owned by the Gram Panchayat is called 'common property resource'.

e. **Area under miscellaneous tree crops and groves** - (which is not included in the net sown area) This category includes the land on which there are gardens and fruit trees. Most of this type of land is in the private ownership of individuals.

f. **Culturable waste land** - The land which is fallow or uncultivated for the last five years or more is included in this category. It can be improved and made cultivable by land reclamation techniques.

g. **Current fallow**- The land which remains uncultivated for one agricultural year or less is called current fallow. Keeping land fallow is a cultural practice to maintain the quality of the land. By this method, the depleted fertility or nutrition of the land returns naturally.

h. **Ancient fallow**- This is also cultivable land which remains uncultivated for more than one year but less than five years. If a land remains uncultivated for more than five years, then it is included in the cultivable wasteland category.

i. **Net area sown**- The land on which crops are grown and harvested is called net sown area.

j. **Gross sown area**- Cultivable wasteland, fallow land, and net sown area together form the gross sown area.

4. Name land use categories that have registered an increase in their reporting area.

Three land uses categories have registered an increase. They are

1) Area under non-agricultural uses:

a) The rate of increase is the highest in case of area under non-agricultural uses. This is due to the increase in demand for land for industrial, infrastructural facilities and services.

b) Expansion of area under both urban and rural settlements.

c) Thus, the wastelands and agricultural land are put under non-agricultural uses.

2) Area under forest: The increase in the area under forest is due to increase in the demarcated area under forest.

3) Area under current fallow: The area under current fallow fluctuates over years, depending on the variability of rainfall and cropping cycles.

5. Name land use categories that have registered a decrease in reporting area.

A. **Area under barren, wasteland and culturable wasteland**: Is due to increase in the pressure on land for both the agricultural and nonagricultural uses.

B. **Net sown area:** Is due to the increases in area under non-agricultural use. The agricultural land is put under buildings and factories.

C. **Pastures and grazing lands:** Is due to expansion of cultivation on pasture lands.

6. What are common property resources?

a) Land under Gram Panchayat is called common property resources.

b) It includes pastures for animals, wood for fuel, fruits, medicinal plants etc.

c) Rural aquatic areas come under it.

d) Economically weak farmers and women get its benefit.

e) These resources give importance to social forestry.

7. Explain the importance of land resource to the livelihood of the people depending on agriculture.

Land resource is more important to the people whose livelihood depend on agriculture:

a) Agriculture output purely depends on land resource. Thus, lack of access to land increases incidence of poverty in rural areas.

b) Quality of land has a direct bearing on the productivity of agriculture, which is not true for other activities.

c) In rural areas, land ownership has a social value and serves as a security for credit, natural hazards or life contingencies, and also adds to the social status.

8. What is land saving technology?

a. The possibilities of increasing the net sown area in India are limited. Hence, it is very important to develop land saving technology.

b. The productivity of a particular crop per unit land can be increased by land saving technology.

c. Intensive land use in an agricultural year can increase the production of crops.

d. With increased production, the demand for workers also increases, which can reduce unemployment.

9. What is cropping intensity? Why is there a need to adopt an intensive agricultural policy in a country like India?

a. There is a shortage of land and an excess of labour in the country.

b. In such a situation, crop intensity is not only required for land use, but it is also necessary to reduce economic problems like unemployment in rural areas.

c. It is calculated as follows-

   Agricultural intensity = Gross sown area / Net sown area x 100

10. Explain the three distinct crop seasons in northern and interior parts of India. Name two crops grown in the each season.

There are three distinct crop seasons in northern India:

1) The Kharif season:

a) It largely begins with onset of Southwest Monsoon in May-June and ends in September-October.

b) Cultivation of **tropical crops** such as rice, cotton, jute, jowar, bajra and tur is done.

2) The rabi season:

a) It begins with the beginning of winter in October-November and ends in March-April.

b) The low temperature conditions during this season facilitate the cultivation of **temperate and subtropical crops**.

c) Crops such as wheat, gram and mustard are grown.

3) Zaid season:

a) It is a short duration summer cropping season in April and May.

b) It begins after harvesting of Rabi crops.

c) The cultivation of watermelons, cucumbers, vegetables and fodder crops during this season is done on irrigated lands.

11. Explain why in southern parts of India same crops can be grown thrice in a year.

In southern India the temperature remains high throughout the year. It is suitable for growing tropical crops during any period in the year. Thus, in this region same tropical crops can be grown thrice in an agricultural year.

12. **What are the two types of farming classified on the basis of main source of moisture for the crops? Give differences between the two.**

Irrigated farming and **Rainfed farming** are the two types of farming classified on the basis of main source of moisture for the crops. Both differ in terms of nature of irrigation and the objective of irrigation:

A.   Rainfed farming also known as Protective farming:

a. The objective of protective irrigation is to protect the crops from adverse effects of lack of soil moisture.

b. Irrigation acts as an additional source of water over and above the rainfall.

c. The strategy of this kind of irrigation is to provide soil moisture to maximum possible area.

B. Irrigated farming also known as Productive irrigation:

a. It is meant to provide sufficient soil moisture in the cropping season.

b. It is done to achieve high productivity.

c. In such irrigation the water input per unit area of cultivated land is higher than protective irrigation.

13. **What are the two types of rainfed farming? Explain the differences between the two types of rainfed farming.**

Rainfed farming is classified into **dryland farming** and **wetland farming.**

a) The dryland farming is largely confined to the regions having annual rainfall less than 75 cm whereas in wetland farming the rainfall is in excess of soil moisture requirement of plants during rainy season.

b) In dryland farming regions hardy and drought resistant crops such as ragi, bajra, moong, gram and guar (fodder crops) are grown whereas in wetland farming regions various water intensive crops such as rice, jute and sugarcane are grown.

c) In dryland farming farmers practise various measures of soil moisture conservation and rain water harvesting whereas in wetland farming practise aquaculture in the fresh water bodies.

d) Dryland farming regions face problems of deficient soil moisture whereas wetland farming regions may face flood and soil erosion hazards.

14. Describe the conditions, area and production of paddy in India.

a. Most important food crop of India, tropical humid crop.

b. In the Himalayas and the north-western parts of the country, it is grown as a Kharif crop in the south-west monsoon season.

c. It has more than 3000 varieties which are grown in different agro-climatic regions.

d. "Aus. Aman, Boro varieties are sown in one agricultural year in West Bengal.

e. India produces 22.07 percent of the world's rice and after China, India ranks second in the world.

f. Rice is sown on ¼ of the total sown area of the country.

g. West Bengal is the most producing state, other major states - Bihar, UP, Haryana, Punjab.

15. Describe the conditions, area and production of wheat in India.

a. Wheat is temperate and babi crop.

b. Highest production in UP. Punjab, Haryana othr leading states.

c. 85% area in northern India, 14% of total sown area.

d. 12.8% of the world, second highest producing country.

e. Per capita productivity of Punjab and Haryana is high.

f. High in areas with irrigation facilities.

16. Describe the conditions, area and production of Maize in India.

a. Maize is a food and fodder crop.

b. It is grown in low quality soil and semi-arid climate.

c. It is sown in only 3.6 percent of the total sown area.

d. Its yield is more than that of coarse grains.

e. Maize cultivation is not concentrated in any particular area. It is sown in almost all parts eastern and north-eastern India.

f. The major producing states are Karnataka, Madhya Pradesh, Bihar, Andhra Pradesh, Telangana, Rajasthan and UP.

g. Its yield is more in the southern states which decreases towards the central parts.

17. Describe the conditions, area and production of Jowar in India.

a. Jowar is the main coarse grain which is sown on 5.3% of the total sown area.

b. It is the main food crop of the semi-arid areas of South and Central India.

c. The state of Maharashtra alone produces more than half of the country's jowar.

d. In the southern states it is sown in both Kharif & Rabi seasons.

e. In North India it is a Kharif crop and is mainly grown as a fodder crop.

f. It is a rain-fed crop in South of Vindhyachal and its productivity is low here.

g. The major jowar producing states are Karnataka, Madhya Pradesh, Andhra Pradesh and Telangana.

18. Describe the conditions, area and production of Bajra in India.

a. Bajra is grown in hot and dry climate in western and n-w parts.

b. This crop is able to tolerate dry spells and drought.

c. It is grown as a single or mixed crop.

d. This crop is grown 5.2% of the total sown area of the country.

e. Being a rain dependent crop, its productivity in Rajasthan is low and has high fluctuations.

f. The arrival of drought resistant varieties and expansion of irrigation facilities have increased the yield of this crop.

g. Major producing states are Maharashtra, Gujarat, Uttar Pradesh, Rajasthan and Haryana.

19. What is the importance of pulses in agriculture?

a) Being a rich source of protein, pulses are an important component of vegetarian diet.

b) These are leguminous crops which increase the natural fertility of soil by nitrogen fixation.

c) India is a major producer of pulses. About 11% of the total sown area of the country is under pulses.

d) Being a rain-fed crop in dry areas, productivity is low and annual fluctuations are seen in it.

e) Gram and pigeon pea are the main pulses of India.

f) In the country, pulses are mostly cultivated in the Deccan plateau, central plateau regions and dry regions of the North-West.

20. Describe the conditions, area and production of Gram and Tur (Arhar) in India.

1. Gram

a. Gram is a crop of subtropical regions which is mainly rain-fed crop.

b. It is sown in the Rabi season in the central, western and north-western parts of the country.

c. With the advent of Green Revolution in Haryana, Punjab and northern Rajasthan, the crop areas of gram have decreased.

d. Gram is cultivated on only 2.8 percent of the total sown area of the country.

e. The major producing states are Madhya Pradesh, Uttar Pradesh, Maharashtra, Andhra Pradesh, Telangana and Rajasthan.

2. Tur (Arhar)

a. Arhar (tur) is the second major pulse crop of the country.

b. It is also known as red gram and pigeon pea.

c. It is sown on rain-fed land in the dry parts of the central and southern states of the country.

d. It is cultivated on about 2% of the total sown area of India.

e. About one-third of the total production of tur in the country comes from Maharashtra alone.

21. Why are oilseeds crops are important in Indian agriculture.

a) Oilseeds are cultivated for extracting edible oil.

b) Malwa plateau, Marathwada, Gujarat, dry parts of Rajasthan, Telangana and **Rayalaseema region of Andhra Pradesh** are the major oilseed producing areas of India.

c) Oilseed crops are sown on about 14% of the total cropped area of the country.

d) Major oilseed crops include groundnut, rapeseed, mustard, soybean and sunflower.

22. Describe the production, area and conditions of groundnut as an oilseed in India.

a) India produces 18.8% of the world's peanuts.

b) In South India, it is sown during the Rabi season.

c) It covers 3.6% of the country's total cropped area.

d) Where the crop is partially irrigated, its yield is relatively high such as in Tamilnadu.

e) Gujarat, Rajasthan, Tamil Nadu, Andhra Pradesh are its leading producing states.

23. Describe the production, area and conditions of mustard as an oilseed in India.

a) Mustard includes many oilseeds, such as rye, mustard, toria and taramira etc.

b) These are subtropical crops and are sown in the Rabi season in central and north-western parts of India.

c) These crops cannot tolerate frost and there is annual fluctuation in their production.

d) They are sown on only about 2.5 percent of the total cropped area of the country.

e) One-third of their production comes from Rajasthan.

24. Describe the production, area and conditions of Soyabean and Sunflower as an important oilseed in India.

1. Soybean:

a. Soybean is mostly grown in MP and Maharashtra.

b. Together both the states produce about 90% of the country's soybean.

2. Sunflower:
   a. Sunflower crop is concentrated in Rajasthan, Karnataka, Andhra Pradesh, Telangana and adjoining parts of Maharashtra.
   b. It is a minor crop in the northern parts of the country but its production is high in irrigated areas.

25. Describe the production, area, conditions and importance of Cotton as an important fibre crop in India.
   a) Cotton is a tropical crop which is sown in the Kharif season in the semi-arid parts of the country.
   b) India produces both short-staple (Indian) and long-staple (American) cotton.
   c) American cotton is called 'Narma' in the north-western part of the country.
   d) India ranks second in the world after China in the production of cotton, it is sown on about 4.7% area in the country.
   e) The sky should be cloudless at the time of flowering of cotton.
   f) There are three main cotton producing areas - Punjab, Haryana and Northern Rajasthan in North-West India; Gujarat and Maharashtra in the West; and the plateau regions of Telangana, Karnataka and Tamil Nadu in the South.
   g) The per hectare production of cotton is higher in the irrigation-rich north-western parts of the country.
   h) Leading producing states are Gujarat, Maharashtra, Telangana, Andhra Pradesh, Punjab & Haryana.

26. Discribe that jute remains a major crop in some areas even though the main production areas are outside the country.
   a. India produces about 60 percent of the world's jute.
   b. It is a commercial crop of W. Bengal & its adjacent parts.
   c. It is sown on 0.5% of the total cropped area of the country.
   d. West Bengal produces 3/4th of the country's production.
   e. Bihar and Assam are other jute producing areas.
   f. Jute is used in making coarse clothes, bags, sacks and other decorative items.

27. Describe the production, area, conditions and importance of tea as an important cash and plantation crop in India.

a. Tea is a plantation crop which is used as a beverage.

b. Tea leaves are rich in caffeine and tannin.

c. India is the leading producer of tea and produces about 21.22 percent of the world's tea.

d. Tea cultivation in India began in 1840 in the Brahmaputra Valley of Assam.

e. Tea is cultivated on 53.2 acres of Assam, more than half of the country's total production is produced in Assam.

f. It is cultivated on the lower slopes of Darjeeling, Jalpaiguri, Cooch Behar (WB), Nilgiri and Cardamom Hills.

g. Among tea-exporting countries, India ranks second in the world after China.

28. Describe the production, area, conditions and importance of Coffee as an important cash and plantation crop in India.

a. There are three varieties of coffee - Arabica, Robusta and Liberica.

b. India produces mostly the best quality 'Arabica' coffee, which is in great demand in the international market.

c. Coffee is a tropical plantation crop. Its seeds are roasted and ground and used as a beverage.

d. India produces only 3.17 percent of the world's coffee and ranks eighth in the world.

e. More than 2/3 of the country's total coffee production comes from the state of Karnataka alone.

29. Describe the production, area, conditions and importance of sugarcane as an important cash crop in india.

a. Sugarcane is a tropical crop, which is cultivated on only 2.4% of the total crop area.

b. India is the second largest sugarcane producing country after Brazil and produces 19.76% of sugarcane.

c. It can be sown only in humid and sub-humid climate areas under rain dependent conditions.

d. The Gangetic-Indus plains, Maharashtra in the west, Gujarat and Karnataka, Tamil Nadu in the south are the major sugarcane producing states.

e. Uttar Pradesh produces 40 percent of the country's sugarcane.

30. What steps did the government took to remove the problems of Indian agriculture?

a. Before independence, Indian agriculture was a subsistence economy. After independence, the immediate objective of the government was to increase the production of food grains, for which the following measures were adopted:

   i. Growing food grains in place of commercial crops.

   ii. Increasing agricultural intensity.

   iii. Converting cultivable barren and fallow lands into agricultural land.

b. Initially, this policy increased the production of food grains, but by the end of the 1950s, agricultural production stagnated. To overcome this problem, Intensive Agricultural District Program (IADP) & Intensive Agricultural Area Program (IAAP) were started.

c. In the mid-1960s, the unprecedented increase in the production of food grains with chemical fertilizers in the irrigated areas of the northwestern states in the form of HYV varieties of wheat (Mexico) and rice (Philippines) and package technology is known as the 'Green Revolution'.

d. Planning Commission started agro-climatic planning in 1988 to promote regional balance in agricultural development. It also emphasized on the development of resources for the development of agriculture, animal husbandry & aquaculture.

e. The liberalization policy of the 1990s have also influenced Indian agricultural development.

f. Programs like Kisan Credit Card, Crop insurance policies strengthened the farmers economically.

g. Through the Minimum Support Price Scheme, farmers can get the minimum purchase price of their crops.

31. **Mention the advantages and disadvantages of Green Revolution.**

    Green Revolution is called the unprecedented increase in food grains, its advantages and disadvantages are as follows-

    A. Advantages of Green Revolution-
    1. In the 1960s, HYV seeds of wheat (Mexico) and rice (Philippines) were developed.
    2. Irrigation and water supply increased production.
    3. Agricultural investment was encouraged.
    4. Agro-based industries developed.
    5. Self-reliance was achieved in foodgrain production.
    6. Agro-climatic planning was started in 1988.

    B. Disadvantages of Green Revolution-
    1. It was limited to irrigated areas only.
    2. Only wheat and rice production could be promoted.
    3. Production of wheat, paddy, cotton etc. in place of traditional crops.
    4. Regional imbalance increased. 5. Rich farmers became richer and poor farmers were not able to get much benefit, due to which social inequality increased.

32. **National Mission for Sustainable Agriculture (NMSA).**
    a. The National Mission for Sustainable Agriculture seeks to make agriculture more specialized, sustainable, remunerative and climate-friendly.
    b. It will focus on expanding water use efficiency, soil health management and resource conservation, etc., so that agricultural productivity can be increased in rain-fed areas.
    c. For this, location-specific integrated/holistic farming systems will be promoted.
    d. Natural resources will be conserved through appropriate soil and moisture conservation measures.
    e. The government is promoting organic farming in the country through schemes like Paramparagat Krishi Vikas Yojana (PKVY) and Rashtriya Krishi Vikas Yojana (RKVY).

33. What is Farmer's Portal of India?

a. Kisan Portal is a platform for farmers to search for any information related to agriculture.

b. Detailed information is provided on farmers' insurance, agricultural storage, crops, extension activities, seeds, pesticides, agricultural machinery, etc.

c. Details of fertilizers, market price, packages and practices, programmes, welfare schemes are also given.

d. Block level details of soil fertility, storage, insurance, training etc. are available in an interactive map.

e. Users can also download farm friendly handbooks, scheme guidelines etc.

34. How Technology helped in growth of Agricultural Output?

There has been a significant increase in agricultural output due to the improvement in technolog as –

a. This provided the basis for the introduction of modern agricultural technology, such as high-yielding varieties of seeds, chemical fertilizers, pesticides and agricultural machinery.

b. The increase in resources has also led to an increase in the net irrigated area in the country.

c. Modern agricultural technology has spread very rapidly in different regions of the country.

d. The consumption of chemical fertilizers has increased 15 times since the mid-sixties.

e. High-yielding varieties are highly susceptible to pests and diseases, so the use of pesticides has increased considerably since the 1960s.

35. Expain the problems of Indian agriculture.

1. **Dependence on irregular monsoon**- Only one third of the agricultural area in India is irrigated, the production of crops in the remaining agricultural area is directly dependent on rain. The uncertainty and irregularity of the south-west monsoon

affects the canal water supply for irrigation. Drought and flood remain the twin crises of Indian agriculture.

2. **Low productivity**- In comparison to the international level, the productivity of crops and the yield per hectare in India is less than that of America, Russia and Japan.

3. **Indebtedness and lack of financial resources**- Modern agriculture is very costly. The agricultural savings of marginal and small farmers are very low. Due to the decreasing income from agriculture and crop failure, they are getting trapped in the debt trap.

4. **Small and fragmented farms**- The number of marginal and small farmers in India is more than 60% and due to increasing population, the average size of these holdings is shrinking even more.

5. **Underemployment**- Underemployment is found on a large scale in Indian agriculture, especially in non-irrigated areas. There is seasonal unemployment in these areas which lasts for 4 to 8 months. Hence, people engaged in agriculture do not get the opportunity to work throughout the year.

6. **Other problems**-
   i. Lack of land reforms
   ii. Degradation of cultivable land
   iii. Barren land and water erosion due to soil salinity
   iv. Excessive use of pesticides causing toxic elements to dissolve in the soil profile.
   v. Lack of fertility in the soil due to reduction in fallow land

7. Thus, most of the agricultural problems of the country are regional, however, some problems are universal, which include physical barriers to institutional barriers.

Objectives

1. Which of the following crops is not grown in dry agriculture?
   a) Ragi
   b) Groundnut
   c) Sorghum
   d) Jute

2. Where farmers grow 3 varieties of paddy in an agricultural year?
   a) Assam
   b) West Bengal
   c) Orissa
   d) Haryana

3. Which of the following is not a land use category?
   a) Fallow land
   b) Net sown area
   c) Marginal land
   d) Cultivable wasteland

4. Which one is a varity of coffee?
   a) Arebica
   b) Nirma
   c) Aman
   d) Aus

5. Were high yielding varieties of wheat and rice developed?
   a) Japan and Australia
   b) Mexico and Philippines
   c) USA and Japan
   d) Mexico and Singapore

6. Which crop is a food and fooder crop both?
   a) Peddy
   b) Maize
   c) Bajra
   d) Cotton

7. When Planning Commission started agro-climatic planning?
   a) 1968
   b) 1978
   c) 1988
   d)1998

8. What is the position of India in paddy production in the world?
   a) First
   b) Second
   c) Third
   d) Fourth

9. Oilseed producing Rayalseema region located in which state?
   a) Andhra Pradesh
   b) Rajasthan
   c) Telangana
   d) Gujrat

10. Which is not a Kharif crop in North India?
    a) Maize
    b) Mustard
    c) Groundnut
    d) Cotton

11. Dry land farming confined mainly where rainfall is less than
    a) 150 cm
    b) 100 cm
    c) 75 cm
    d) 50 cm

Answers: 1-d, 2-b, 3-c, 4-a, 5-b, 6-b, 7-c, 8-b, 9-a, 10-b, 11-c

CHAPTER 4 - WATER RESOURCES

1. Describe the availability of water resources in India.

a) India have about 4 per cent of the world's water resources.

b) The total water available from precipitation in the country in a year is about 4,000 cubic km.

c) The availability from surface water and replenishable groundwater is 1,869 cubic km.

d) Out of this only 60 per cent can be put to beneficial uses.

e) Thus, the total utilizable water resource in the country is only 1,122 cubic km.

2. What are the uses of lagoons and backwaters?

a. The coastline is indented, which leads to the formation of lagoon lakes.

b. Kerala, Orissa, West Bengal have more backwater resources.

c. They have saline water which helps in fish farming and coconut production.

d. Backwaters are also useful for water transport.

e. On the west coast, these backwater lakes are called "**Kayaal**".

3. Describe the features of surface water distribution in India.

There are four major sources of surface water. These are rivers, lakes, ponds, and tanks.

a) In the country, there are about 10,360 rivers and tributaries longer than 1.6 km each.

b) The average annual flow in all river basins is 1,869 cubic km.

c) Only 32 per cent of the available surface water can be utilized due to topographical, hydrological and other constraints.

d) The Ganga and the Brahmaputra River have 60 % of the total water resource in India.

4. Describe the features of ground water distribution in India.

a) Groundwater resources in the country are about 432 cubic km.

b) The Ganga and the Brahmaputra basins together have about 46 per cent of the total replenishable groundwater resources.

c) The level of groundwater utilisation is high in the river basins in north-western region and south India.

d) The groundwater utilisation is very high in the states of Punjab, Haryana, Rajasthan, and Tamil Nadu.

e) States like Chhattisgarh, Orissa, Kerala, etc. have small groundwater utilization.

5. State important uses of water resources in India.

Water resources are used for:

A. **Irrigation in Agriculture**:

a) India's water demand is dominated by irrigational needs.

b) 89 per cent of the Surface water is used for irrigation.

c) 92 per cent of the Ground water is used for irrigation.

B. **Industries**: Its share is limited to 2 per cent of the surface water and 5 per cent of the ground-water.

C. **Domestic**: More of surface water i.e. 9% is used in domestic sector as compared to groundwater i.e. 3%.

6. Why the demand of water for irrigation is high in India.

Major Use of water is for irrigation in India. It is due to following reasons:

A. **Variability in rainfall**:

a) **The spatial distribution** of rainfall is uneven. Most parts of India such as north-west and Deccan plateau remain drought prone due to deficient rainfall. It becomes very difficult to practice agriculture without irrigation.

b) **Seasonal distribution** of rainfall is also uneven. Summer and winter season remain dry. Therefore, in irrigation is required.

B. **Uncertain Rainfall**: Even during rainy season there are breaks in the monsoon therefore in West Bengal and Bihar irrigation is required even during rainy season.

C. **Water requirements** of certain crops such as jute, sugarcane, rice, is very high therefore the demand for irrigation is high.

D. Provision of irrigation makes **multiple cropping** possible.

E. **Agriculture productivity** is high in irrigated fields as compared to un-irrigated land.

F. **Use of high yielding seeds and fertilizers** have made the irrigation essential.

G. **Green revolution** in Punjab and Haryana was successful due to irrigation.

H. **Location:** India is located in the tropical and sub-tropical region evapo-transpiration is also high.

7. What are the implications of over using of ground water resources?

The over-use of ground water resources in dry and drought prone areas has led to:

a) Decline in ground water table in Rajasthan and Gujarat.

b) Increased fluoride concentration in ground-water due to over withdrawal in Maharashtra and Rajasthan.

c) Increase in concentration of arsenic in West Bengal and Bihar.

d) Increased salinity in the soil in Punjab and Haryana.

8. What are the emerging water problems in India?

a) Water resources in India face many problems such as problem of availability and quality.

b) Problems of availability: Per capita availability of water is decreasing day by day. Its supply also varies with seasons.

c) Problems of quality: The quality of water is decreasing due to water pollution. Domestic wastewater, industrial effluents and chemicals used in agriculture pollute water.

9. What are the major causes of deterioration of water quality in India?

The quality of surface water and ground water decreases due to:

a. Foreign matters such as micro-organisms, chemicals, industrial and other wastes.

b. Discharge of domestic and industrial wastewater from cities and towns without treatment in rivers and lakes.

c. Excessive use of fertilizers, insecticides, and pesticides in agricultural fields.

d. Seepage of these pollutants underground.

10. **Why conservation and management of water resource is necessary in India?**

    Water conservation and management is necessary in India due to following reasons:

    c. The availability of fresh water in many parts of our country is declining.

    d. The demand for water is increasing rapidly.

    e. Many areas face shortage of water.

    f. Sustainable development can only be achieved by water management.

    g. Its quality is getting lower by the human activities.

    h. Water available from sea/ocean is negligible due to high cost of de-salinisation. Under such view conservation of water is necessary.

11. **What steps has to take to conserve water resources in India?**

    Availability of water resources can be increased & conserved by:

    a. Keeping water resource **free from pollution** by treating the wastewater from cities and industries.

    b. Encouraging **recycling and reuse of water** for long run.

    c. **Watershed development**: Scientifically managing the water resource of all river watersheds.

    d. **Rainwater harvesting**: Collecting rainwater and stopping it from draining off.

12. **Mention the main causes of water pollution in rivers and measures to prevent them.**

    Water pollution in these rivers is caused by:

    i. Most polluted rivers are Ganga, Yamuna, Sabarmati, Gomti.

    ii. The intensive use of river water for irrigation, drinking, domestic and industrial purposes.

    iii. The drains carrying agricultural (fertilisers and insecticides), domestic (solid and liquid wastes), and industrial effluents.

    iv. The Low flow of water during the summer season.

    v. The Organic and bacterial contaminations.

The water pollution in these rivers can be prevented by:

a. The legislative provisions such as the Water Acts and Environment Protection Acts must be implemented effectively.

b. Generating public awareness and action about importance of water and impacts of water pollution.

c. **Recycle and Reuse** of low-quality water for industrial purposes and fire fighting to reduce their water cost.

d. urban areas water after bathing and washing utensils can be used for gardening. Water used for washing vehicle can also be used for gardening.

e. This would conserve fresh water for drinking purposes.

13. What is watershed management?

a. Watershed management refers to efficient management and conservation of surface and ground water resources and other natural and human resources within the watershed..

b. It includes arresting runoff and water recharging and Its main objective is to create balance between natural resources and society. The success of watershed management mainly depends on community cooperation.

c. The central, state governments and non-governmental organizations (NGOs) have launched several watershed development and management programmes in the country.

d. '**Hariyali**' is a watershed development project initiated by the central government which aims to enable the rural population to conserve water for drinking, irrigation, fisheries and afforestation. The project is being executed by gram panchayats with the cooperation of the people.

e. Various water harvesting structures have been constructed with the cooperation of people under Neeru-Meeru (Andhra Pradesh) and Aravari Pani Sansad (Alwar, Rajasthan).

f. There is a need to create awareness among the people of the country by telling them the benefits of watershed development and management.

14. **How Ralegaon Siddhi Village is become best example of Watershed Development.**
   i.   Ralegaon Siddhi, Ahmednagar (Maharashtra) is a great example of watershed development.
   ii. Earlier this village was plagued by unemployment and illegal liquor trade.
   iii. Reduced economic dependence on the government by socializing the cost of projects.
   iv. Developed groundwater capacity by improving ponds and stopping flowing water.
   v.   Spread awareness about prohibition by forming a youth group Tarun Mandal.
   vi. Encouraged crops that required less water.
   vii. Established local justice panchayat system which strengthened the justice system.
   viii. Landless farmers got employment & unemployment reduced.
   ix. By constructing a school building using only village resources, the people of the village were made to feel self-reliant.

15. **What are the benefits of rainwater harvesting? What are the methods of rainwater harvesting?**
   i.   Rainwater harvesting is a method of stopping and collecting the flowing rainwater for various uses, which also recharges the groundwater.
   ii. It is a low cost and eco-friendly method by which rainwater is collected in tube wells, pits and wells to conserve the water.
   iii. Rainwater harvesting increases the availability of water, prevents the depletion of groundwater level, improves the quality of groundwater by reducing contaminants like fluoride and nitrates.
   iv. Prevents soil erosion and floods and the entry of saline water in coastal areas.
   v.   Urban areas can also benefit from rainwater harvesting because the water use demand here is more than the capacity of water reserves.

16. What are the methods of rainwater harvesting?

i. Various communities in the country collect rainwater by various methods.

ii. In Rajasthan, rainwater harvesting is done through cisterns or tanks, which are constructed near the house or village to collect rainwater.

iii. By constructing check dams, reducing silt and weeds of lakes and ponds etc.

iv. Rainwater can be collected by collecting it on the roof of houses and storing it underground.

17. Expalin the objectives of National Water Policy 2002.

i. In the National Water Policy 2002, water allocation priorities have been specified for drinking water, irrigation, hydropower, boating, industrial and other uses.

ii. Inclusion of drinking water component in irrigation and multipurpose projects, where there is no alternative source of drinking water.

iii. Providing drinking water to all human beings and animals will be the first priority.

iv. Measures should be taken to limit and regulate the exploitation of groundwater.

v. There should be regular testing for the quality of both surface and groundwater.

vi. Efficiency should be improved in all the various uses of water.

vii. Awareness should be developed for water as a scarce resource.

viii. Conservation consciousness should be increased through educational exchange, initiatives, motivations and indexes.

18. What are the objectives of Jal Kranti Abhiyan?

i. This scheme was started by the Indian Government in 2015-16.

ii. The objective of the campaign is to ensure availability of water per person.

iii. The most water deficient village of the country will be selected as **Jal Gram**.

iv. 1000 hectare command area will be identified in this campaign.

v. Another major objective of this campaign is to reduce water pollution.

vi. Print and tele media will be used for public awareness.

vii. Food and livelihood will be provided through water security.

19. **Main objectives of Pradhan Mantri Krishi Sinchayee Yojana.**

i. Pradhan Mantri Krishi Sinchayee Yojana has been launched by the Central Government during 2015-16.

ii. Its' overarching vision to ensure access to some means of protective irrigation for all agricultural farms in the country, thus bringing much desired rural prosperity.

iii. **Har khet ko pani**- To enhance the physical access of water on the farm and expand cultivable area under assured irrigation.

iv. To promote integration of water source, distribution and its efficient use, to make best use of water through appropriate technologies and practices.

v. **Per drope more crop**- To improve on-farm water use efficiency to reduce wastage and increase availability both in duration and exent irrigation and other water saving technologies.

vi. To introduce sustainable water conservation practices.

vii. To ensure the integrated development of rain-fed areas using the waters held approach towards soil and water conservation, regeration of ground water, providing livelihood options, etc.

20. **Main objectives of Atal Bhujal Yojana (Atal Jal).**

i. One of the key aspects of ATAL JAL is to bring in behavioural changes in the community, from the prevailing attitude of consumption to conservation and smart water management.

ii. Atal Bhujal Yojana (Atal Jal) is being implemented in 8220 water stressed Gram Panchayats of 229 administrative blocks/ talukas in 80 districts.

iii. It is introduced in seven states, viz. Gujarat, Haryana, Karnataka, Madhya Pradesh, Maharashtra, Rajasthan & UP.

iv. The selected States account for about 37 per cent of the total number of water-stressed (over-exploited, critical and semi-critical) blocks in India.

<u>Objectives</u>

1. Which of the following type of resource is water?
   a) Abiotic resource
   b) Biotic resource
   c) Non-renewable resource
   d) Cyclic resource

2. In which of the following South Indian states, ground water use (in %) is more than its total ground water potential?
   a) Tamil Nadu
   b) Andhra Pradesh
   c) Karnataka
   d) Kerala

3. Which of the following sectors accounts for the highest proportion of total water used in the country?
   a) Irrigation
   b) Domestic use
   c) Industry
   d) None of these

4. Which river comes under 'East flowing river group-2'?
   a) Swarnarekha
   b) Mahanadi
   c) Krishna
   d) Kaveri

5. Which one of the following is not a source of surface water?
   a) Rivers
   b) Lakes
   c) Ground water
   d) Ponds

6. Environment Protection Act implemented in which year?
   a) 1975
   b) 1980
   c) 1986
   d) 1992

7. Which watershed development project sponsored by the Central Government?
   a) Haryali
   b) Neeru-Meeru
   c) Arvary Pani Sansad
   d) Ralegan Siddhi

<u>**Answers:**</u> **1-d, 2-a, 3-a, 4-d, 5-c, 6-c, 7-a**

CHAPTER 5 - MINERAL & ENERGY RESOURCES

1. **What is a mineral? What are the characteristics of minerals?**

   A mineral is a natural substance of organic or inorganic origin with certain chemical and physical properties /characteristics. Its main characteristics are as follows

   a) Mineral resources provide the necessary base and raw material for industrial development.

   b) Minerals are unevenly distributed. Minerals of higher quality are found in lesser quantities than minerals of lower quality.

   c) They can be exhausted with time. They take many years to form.

   d) Most of the minerals are not replenishable. Hence their conservation is necessary.

2. **Mention the types of mineral resources.**

   On the basis of chemical and physical properties, minerals are divided into two major categories-

   1. **Metallic minerals** – The minerals which are the source of metal are metallic minerals, such as iron ore, copper, gold etc. These minerals are divided into two categories-

      a) Ferrous minerals – The minerals which contain iron element are called ferrous minerals; such as iron, manganese etc.

      b) Non-ferrous minerals – The minerals which do not contain iron are called non-ferrous minerals; such as copper, bauxite etc.

   2. **Non-metallic minerals** – The minerals which are made of organic or inorganic minerals are called non-metallic minerals, such as coal, mica, limestone etc.

      a) Organic minerals – The minerals which are obtained from animal and plant organisms buried in the earth; are called organic minerals. These are also called fossil fuels; such as coal, natural gas, petroleum etc.

      b) Inorganic Minerals- Minerals which contain neither carbon nor iron elements are called inorganic minerals, such as mica, limestone, graphite, etc.

3. **What is the distribution pattern of minerals (mineral belt) in India?**

    India is rich in various types of minerals due to its diverse geological structure. Minerals in India are mainly concentrated in three broad belts-

    A. North-eastern plateau region

    a) This region includes Chota Nagpur plateau, Orissa plateau, West Bengal and part of Chhattisgarh. Iron ore, coal, bauxite, manganese and mica are the major minerals found.

    b) Due to the availability of the above mentioned major minerals, major iron and steel industries like Bhilai, Bokaro, Jamshedpur, Durgapur etc. are located in this region.

    B. South-western plateau region

    a) Spread in Karnataka, Goa, highlands of Tamil Nadu and Kerala.

    b) Iron ore, manganese, limestone, lignite coal (Niveli) etc.

    c) Atomic minerals like monazite and thorium are also found in Kerala.

    C. North-Western Region

    a) In some parts of Rajasthan and Gujarat.

    b) Copper, Zinc, Granite, Marble, Sandstone, Gypsum (Building Construction), Multani Mitti, Dolomite, Petroleum, Salt, Limestone (Cement Industry), etc.

    D. Other Mineral Belts

    a) Himalayan belt is another mineral belt, where copper, lead, zinc, cobalt and gemstone are found. These are found in both the eastern and western parts.

    b) There are deposits of mineral oils in Assam valley.

    c) Offshore (Mumbai High) are rich in mineral oil resources.

4. **Present the distribution of major iron ores in India.**

    a) Hematite and magnetite are the largest reserves of high-grade iron ore.

    b) Odisha, Jharkhand, Chhattisgarh, Karnataka etc. are the major producing states.

c) Sundargarh, Mayurbhanj, Gurumahisni, Sulaypat, Badampahar, Noamundi, Gua are the major mines of Orissa.

d) Bailadila, Dalli, Rajhara, Dantebara are the major mines of Chhattisgarh.

e) Sandur-Hospete, Baba-Budan, Kudremukh are the major mines of Karnataka.

f) Chandrapur, Bhandara, Ratnagiri are the major iron-ore areas in Maharashtra.

g) Karimganj, Warangal (Telangana), Kurnool, Kadapa, Anantapur (Andhra Pradesh) and Salem (Tamil Nadu) are other major iron-ore areas.

5. Present the main distribution of manganese in India.

a) Manganese is used in smelting and manufacturing of iron ore.

b) Manganese deposits are found in almost all geological formations in India.

c) Orissa is the leading producer of manganese. Bonai, Kendujhar, Sundargarh, Koraput, Kalahandi, Bolangir, Gangpur are the major manganese mines of Orissa.

d) Bellary, Belgaum, North Kanara, Chikkamangaluru, Shivamogga, Chitradurga, Tumkuru are the major mines of Karnataka.

e) Manganese mines of Maharashtra are unprofitable due to being located far away from steel plants like Nagpur, Bhandara, Ratnagiri etc.

f) In Madhya Pradesh, the belt of manganese extends to Balaghat, Chhindwara, Nimar, Mandla, Jhabua districts.

6. Present the distribution of bauxite in India.

a) Bauxite ore is used in the manufacture of aluminium.

b) It is found mainly in tertiary deposits as well as in coastal areas.

c) Orissa is the largest producer state with Kalahandi, Sambalpur mines.

d) Lohardagga peatlands in Jharkhand have rich deposits of bauxite.

e) Chhattisgarh (Amarkantak Hills), Madhya Pradesh (Katni, Jabalpur, Amarkantak, Maikal Hills, Balaghat), Maharashtra (Colaba, Thane, Ratnagiri, Satara, Pune, Kolhapur), Gujarat (Bhavnagar and Jamnagar) are other bauxite producing states.

7. Give details of distribution of copper in India.

a) Copper is an essential metal for the electrical industry. It is used in making electric motors, transformers and generators etc.

b) Copper is an alloyable, malleable and ductile metal.

c) It is mixed with gold to make ornaments strong.

d) Copper deposits are found in districts like Singhbhum, Hazaribagh (Jharkhand), Balaghat (Madhya Pradesh), Khetri, Jhunjhunu, Alwar, Bhilwara, Udaipur (Rajasthan) etc.

8. Give details of the distribution of mica in India.

a) Mica is a non-metallic mineral used in electrical and electronics industries.

b) It can be cleaved into hard and malleable thin sheets.

c) In India, mica is mainly found in Hazaribagh (Jharkhand), Nellore (Andhra Pradesh), Bhilwara, Udaipur (Rajasthan).

d) The best quality of mica is produced in Nellore district (Andhra Pradesh).

e) It is spread in the form of a wide strip in Jharkhand and Rajasthan.

9. What are energy resources?

a) Mineral fuels produced energy are called energy resources.

b) Energy resources are required in agriculture, industry, transport and other sectors of the economy.

c) These resources classified into renewable and non-renewable.

d) Fossil fuels like coal, petroleum, natural gas etc. and nuclear energy are conventional sources of energy. These conventional sources are exhaustible resources.

e) Solar, wind, water, geothermal, biomass etc. are the main examples of unconventional energy sources.

10. **What is the difference between conventional and unconventional energy sources?**

   A. **Conventional energy sources (non-renewable)-**
   a) These are also called non-renewable energy resources.
   b) These are also known as fossil fuels and are polluting.
   c) These are exhaustible resources.
   d) These resources go through a long process of formation.
   e) These are non-renewable, they get exhausted by repeated use.
   f) Coal, petroleum, natural gas (fossil fuel), nuclear energy etc.

   B. **Non-conventional energy sources (renewable)-**
   a) Only sources of sustainable energy are renewable sources.
   b) These energy sources are more evenly distributed.
   c) These energy sources are environment friendly and do not cause pollution.
   d) Despite high cost, they provide sustainable and cheap energy.
   e) Solar, wind, water, nuclear, geothermal, biomass etc. are the main examples.
   f) Since conventional energy sources are exhaustible resources, conservation of resources is very important. For this, there is a greater need to develop unconventional energy sources for alternative sources of energy.

11. **Write a detailed note on the coal resources of India.**
   a) Coal is mainly used for thermal power generation and smelting of iron ore.
   b) In India, coal is found in the rock sequences of Gondwana and tertiary deposits.
   c) About 80% bituminous type coal deposits are found in India.
   d) The coal area located in Damodar valley is the most important and Jharia is the largest coal area.
   e) Raniganj, Bokaro, Giridih, Singrauli, Korba, Talcher, Singareni etc. are the major coal producing areas.
   f) Lignite (brown) is found in the coastal areas of Tamil Nadu.

12. Write a note on the petroleum resources of India.

a) Petroleum is called liquid gold due to its rarity and diverse uses.

b) It is an essential source of energy for internal combustion fuel of vehicles etc.

c) Its co-products are used in fertilizers, synthetic rubber, synthetic fibres, vaseline, lubricants, wax, soap, cosmetics etc.

d) ONGC was established in 1956 for oil exploration and production.

e) Digboi, Naharkatia, Shivsagar, Moran-Assam, Bombay High, Bassein-Maharashtra, Ankleshwar, Kalol, Mehsana, Navagaon, Kosamba, and Lunej-Gujarat etc. are the major petroleum producing areas.

f) Petroleum is unrefined and full of many impurities, so it cannot be used directly.

g) Based on the need to be refined, two types of oil refineries have been established - production area based (Digboi, Numaligarh, Guwahati, Bongaigaon, Jamnagar) and market based (Barauni, Koyali, Mathura, Panipat, Bina) etc.

13. Comment on the natural gas resources of India.

a) Natural gas is found along with petroleum deposits and is liberated when crude oil is brought to the surface.

b) It is used as industrial fuel, power generation, heating in industries, raw material in petrochemical and fertilizer industries.

c) With the expansion of local city gas distribution (COD) networks, natural gas is also emerging as CNG and PNG as cooking fuel in households.

d) India's major gas reserves are found in the Mumbai High area on the west coast supplemented by the fields found in the Khambhat Basin.

e) Natural gas reserves are found in the Krishna-Godavari Basin on the east coast.

f) The 1,700 km long Hazira-Vijaypur-Jagadishpur (HVJ) gas pipeline constructed by GAIL connects the Mumbai High and Bassein gas fields with various fertilizer, power and industrial complexes in western and northern India.

g) GAIL (India) has laid cross-country natural gas pipeline under 'One Nation One Grid'.

14. Write an essay on solar energy in India.

a) India receives sufficient solar energy between the Equator and the Tropic of Cancer.

b) Solar energy can be produced through photovoltaic and solar-thermal technology.

c) Solar energy is more profitable than other non-renewable energy sources.

d) It is less costly and easy to produce compared to other sources.

e) It is eco friendly and does not cause environmental pollution.

f) It is used in equipment like street lights, motors, crop dryers, cookers etc.

g) There is a lot of potential for the development of solar energy in Gujarat and Rajasthan.

15. Write an essay on wind energy in India.

a) Wind energy is a pollution free & inexhaustible energy source.

b) The technology of converting the kinetic energy of wind into electrical energy through turbine is easy.

c) Sea coasts are favourable places for this, where westerly, terrestrial and sea winds can be used to generate electricity.

d) Rajasthan, Gujarat, Maharashtra, Karnataka are favourable states for wind energy.

e) The import burden value of the country can be reduced by wind energy production.

16. Present an essay on geothermal energy in India.

a) The high temperature heat coming out of magma inside the earth can be converted into electrical energy.

b) Energy can also be generated from the steam of hot water coming out of geyser wells.

c) In India, a geothermal energy plant has been authorized in Manikaran (Himachal Pradesh).

d) Other geothermal energy centers like Tatapani, Puga, Atri, Bakreshwar and Sanota are located in India.

e) Geothermal energy can be developed as an alternative energy source.

17. **Write an essay on tidal and wave energy in India.**

a) Ocean currents are an infinite storehouse of energy.

b) Since the 17th and early 18th centuries, there have been continuous efforts to create energy systems from tidal waves and ocean currents.

c) Large tidal energy and waves are generated in the Gulf of Khambhat and Kutch on the western coast of India.

d) India has great potential for developing tidal energy along the coasts, but it has not been widely used yet.

e) Durgaduani in West Bengal is a major tidal power project in India.

18. **Write an essay on the development of bio-energy in India.**

a) It is obtained from organic products of agricultural residues (bagasse etc.), cow dung, municipal and industrial waste.

b) Thermal energy & gas for cooking can be produced from this.

c) It can reduce waste and also produce energy.

d) It will provide better options for rural areas and increase self-sufficiency which can reduce the pressure on firewood.

e) The bio-energy plant is located in Okhla (New Delhi).

19. **Why is there a need to conserve mineral resources?**

a) Traditional methods of resource use result in large amounts of waste along with other environmental problems, so resource conservation is very important.

b) To conserve non-renewable resources, the use of renewable resources, such as solar energy, wind energy, etc. should be promoted.

c) Metallic minerals should be treated with shale, scrap metals, waste materials should be recycled, etc.

d) Substitutes for metals that are in short supply should be used.

e) Mineral reserves can also be protected by reducing the export of strategic minerals.

Objectives

1. Which of the following is not a ferous-metallic mineral?
   a) Iron
   b) Manganese
   c) Bauxite
   d) Chromite

2. Most of the major minerals are found to the east of the imaginary line joining which cities?
   a) Chennai to Kanpur
   b) Mangalore to Kanpur
   c) Mangalore to Kolkata
   d) Kolkata to Shimla

3. Copper is not used in which of the following?
   a) In the electrical industry
   b) In making electrical wires
   c) In jewellery
   d) In the nuclear energy

4. What is the position of India in Mica production in the world?
   a) First
   b) Second
   c) Third
   d) Fourth

5. Which mineral is used in the manufacture of aluminium?
   a) Manganese
   b) Cobalt
   c) Bauxite
   d) Nickel

6. Which of the following minerals is known as 'Brown Diamond'?
   a) Iron
   b) Manganese
   c) Lignite
   d) Mica

7. 80% of the coal in India is of which type?
   a) Bituminous
   b) Lignite
   c) Hematite
   d) Magnetite

8. Thorium is obtained from monazite and ilmenite in the sand of which coastal region?
   a) Konkan Coast
   b) Malabar Coast
   c) Coromandel Coast
   d) North Circar Coast

9. When was the Atomic Energy Commission established?
   a) 1948
   b) 1954
   c) 1967
   d) 1978

10. Geothermal power plant 'Manikaran' is located in which state?
    a) Chhattisgarh
    b) Jharkhand
    c) Arunachal Pradesh
    d) Himachal Pradesh

11. Which statement/statements is/are correct?
    i. Mumbai High petroleum field was discovered in 1973.
    ii. It is located 160 km from Mumbai coast in the Arabian Sea.
    iii. Production started from here from 1976.
    a) i, ii and iii
    b) i and ii
    c) ii and iii
    d) i and iii

12. Which of the following statements is/are correct?
    i) Hematite, magnetite are types of coal.
    ii) Lignite, bituminous, anthracite are types of iron ore.
    iii) Orissa is producing the most manganese.
    a) i, ii and iii
    b) i and ii
    c) ii and iii
    d) Only iii

13. Which of the following is not a correct match?
    a) Kalpakkam - Tamil Nadu
    b) Narora - Uttar Pradesh
    c) Kaiga - Karnataka
    d) Kakrapara – Maharashtra

14. Which of the following is not a correct match?
    a) Gurumahisani, Badampahar, Bailadila   - Iron-ore
    b) Nellore, Bhilwara, Udaipur   - Mica
    c) Kalol, Naharkatia, Moran   - Petroleum
    d) Khetri, Singhbhum, Hazaribagh   - Bauxite

15. Which of the following is not match correctly?
    a) Rawatbhata – Wind energy
    b) Okhla – Bio energy
    c) Digboi – Petrolium
    d) Khetri - Copper

Answers: 1-c, 2-b, 3-d, 4-a, 5-c, 6-c, 7-a, 8-b, 9-a, 10-d, 11-a, 12-d, 13-d, 14-d, 15-a

Chapter 6: Planning and Sustainable Development in Indian Context

1. What is Planning?

a. Planning is a process of thinking.

b. To prepare the outline of the program.

c. Activities are implemented to fulfill the objectives.

d. Planning is a process of economic development.

e. It is of two types - sectoral and regional.

f. Sectoral planning - is related to the development of social services like agriculture, irrigation, manufacturing, energy, transport and communication.

g. Regional planning - is related to the plan to reduce regional imbalance in backward areas.

2. What is the objective of NITI Aayog?

a. The Commission was formed on 1 Jan 2015 in place of Planning Commission.

b. Its full name is National Institution for Transforming India.

c. To give strategic and technical advice to the central and state governments.

d. To ensure the participation of states in economic policy making.

3. What is the difference between target area and target group planning?

a. Sometimes even the areas rich in resources remain backward.

b. For development, technology and investment are required along with resources.

c. Target area and target group planning was started to remove discrepancies.

d. Target area planning includes command controlled areas, drought prone areas, hilly area development program etc.

e. Target group planning includes Small Farmers Development Institute (SFDA), Marginal Farmers Development Institute (MFDA) etc.

4. **What are the main objectives of the Hill Area Development Program?**

   a. This program was implemented in the fifth five-year plan.

   b. Places more than 600 m high, which are not included in the tribal sub-plan, were included.

   c. It includes 15 districts including Uttarakhand, Cachar, Nilgiri, Darjeeling.

   d. The main objective of this program is that everyone should benefit.

   e. To develop local resources and talents.

   f. Backward areas should not be exploited.

   g. To benefit workers by improving the market system.

   h. To maintain ecological balance.

5. **What are the main objectives of the Drought Prone Area Development Programme?**

   a. This programme was implemented in the Fourth Five Year Plan.

   b. To provide employment in drought-prone areas and to develop means of production.

   c. Other strategies for developing these areas include adopting integrated watershed development programmes at the micro-level.

   d. In the strategy for development of drought-prone areas, the main focus should be on restoration of ecological balance between water, soil, plants, human and animal population.

   e. In 1967, the Planning Commission identified 67 districts (fully or partially) in the country as drought-prone districts.

   f. In 1972, the Irrigation Commission demarcated drought-prone areas by taking the criterion of 30 percent irrigated area.

6. **What are the social benefits of Integrated Tribal Development Programme in Bharmour tribal area?**

   a. Bharmour is located in Chamba district of Himachal Pradesh.

   b. This area is inhabited by the Gaddi tribe who migrate seasonally.

c. Integrated Tribal Development Project (ITDP) was implemented under the Fifth Plan.
d. Transport, communication, agriculture were developed.
e. Social and community services were developed.
f. More emphasis was laid on the development of education, public health, drinking water, roads etc.
g. Literacy improved sex ratio and reduced child marriage.

7. **Define the concept of sustainable development.**
   a. A development which fulfills one's own needs without affecting the fulfillment of the needs of future generations.
   b. The publication of Ehrlich's book 'The Population Bomb' published in 1968 and 'The Limits to Growth' written by Meadows and others in 1972 further deepened the concern of people and especially environmentalists on sustainable development.
   c. In the 1970s, phrases like 'growth with redistribution and growth and equity' were included in the definition of development.
   d. UNO established the World Commission on Environment and Development (WCED) under the chairmanship of Norwegian Prime Minister Garo Harlem Brundtland.
   e. The commission presented its report titled 'Our Common Future' which is also called the Brundtland Report.

8. **What positive impact did the Indira Gandhi Canal Command Area have on irrigation?**
   a. Indira Gandhi Canal, formerly known as Rajasthan Canal. The project conceived by Kuvar Sen in 1948, was started on 31 March 1958.
   b. It originates from the Sutlej river at Harike dam which is about 9060 km. long.
   c. Due to availability of moisture, the land became green due to development of pastures.
   d. Wind erosion decreased and sand deposition decreased.

e. Intensive irrigation increased agricultural and livestock productivity.

f. The sown area expanded and the density of crops increased.

g. Production of wheat, paddy, cotton etc. started increasing.

9. What negative impact did the Indira Gandhi Canal Command Area have on irrigation?

a. Intensive irrigation and excessive use of water caused the problem of water logging and soil salinity.

b. Traditional crops like gram, millet, sorghum, etc. were replaced by wheat, cotton, groundnut and rice.

c. Rich farmers became more prosperous but weak and marginal farmers did not get much benefit. .

10. Suggest measures to promote sustainable development in Indira Gandhi Canal Command Area.

a. Water management policy should be strictly implemented.

b. Water intensive crops should not be grown.

c. Citrus fruits should be cultivated under plantation agriculture.

d. Loss of running water should be prevented.

e. Waterlogged and saline land should be reclaimed.

f. Shelter belt of trees should be developed.

g. Financial assistance should be given to poor and marginal farmers.

h. Agriculture should be linked with other economic activities like animal husbandry, horticulture etc.

<u>Objectives</u>

1. When was NITI Aayog formed?
   a) 1 January 2014   b) 1 July 2014
   c) 1 January 2015   d) 1 July 2015

2. Regional planning is related to-
   a) Development of different sectors of the economy
   b) Regional differences in transport and water systems
   c) Approach to development of a particular region
   d) Development of rural areas

3. ITDP is described in which of the following contexts?
   a) Integrated Tourism Development Programme
   b) Integrated Tribal Development Project
   c) Integrated Travel Development Project
   d) Integrated Tribal Development Programme

4. WECD Commission present its report name?
   a) The Population Bomb
   b) The limits to growth
   c) Our Common Future
   d) Sustainable Report

5. Places at what height are called hilly areas?
   a) Higher than 500 m
   b) Higher than 600 m
   c) Higher than 1000 m
   d) Higher than 1600 m

6. Indira Gandhi Canal originates from which river?
   a) Chenab
   b) Ravi
   c) Sutlej
   d) Jhelum

7. Which tribe resides in the Bharmour region?
   a) Bakarwal
   b) Bhutiya
   c) Gaddis
   d) Tharu

8. Which of the following is not correctly matched?
   a) Hill Area Development Programme   – 4th Five Year Plan
   b) Drought Prone Area Programme   – 4th Five Year Plan
   c) Integrated Tribal Development Project   – 5th Five Year Plan
   d) NITI Aayog   - 2015

9. Which of the following is not included in target area planning?
   a) Indira Gandhi Canal Command Controlled Area
   b) Marginal Farmers Development Institute
   c) Drought Prone Area Development Programme
   d) Hill Area Development Programme

10. Bharmour region is in which state?
    a) Uttrakhand
    b) Punjab
    c) Ladakh
    d) Himachal Pradesh

Answers: 1-c, 2-c, 3-b, 4-c, 5-b, 6-c, 7-c, 8-a, 9-b, 10-d.

CHAPTER 7 - TRANSPORT AND COMMUNICATION

1. How transport and communication important in our lives?

a) Transport takes goods from the places of production to the market, where they are available to consumers.

b) We use physical goods in our daily lives. We also use ideas, philosophy and messages.

c) While communicating through various means, we exchange our ideas, philosophy and messages from one place to another or from one person to another.

d) The use of transport and communication depends on our need to carry a commodity from the place of its availability to the place of its use.

e) Humans use different methods such as rail, road etc. to carry various goods, materials and ideas from one place to another.

2. Mention the different means of transport.

The means of transport can be divided into three main types

A. **Land transport**- Land transport includes road, rail, ropeway, cable, animal, human and pipeline etc.

B. **Water transport**- Water transport is divided into inland and sea route.

C. **Air transport**- Air transport is divided into national and international airways.

3. What is the utility or importance of road transport in India?

i) India's road network is the second largest road network in the world. Its total length is about 56 lakh km.

ii) Here about 85% of passengers and 70% of freight traffic is transported by roads every year.

iii) Road transport is relatively suitable for travelling short distances.

4. Describe the role of roads in the economic development of India.

a) Modern type of road transport was very limited in India before the Second World War. The first serious effort was made in 1943 by making the **'Nagpur Plan'**.

b) After independence, a twenty-year road plan (1961) was started to improve the condition of roads in India. The concentration of roads remained in cities and their surrounding areas. There was almost no connectivity by road with rural and remote areas.

c) **Pradhan Mantri Gramin Sadak Pariyojana** - The special provision of this project is to connect rural areas and villages to cities, so that every village of the country can be connected to major cities by paved roads (roads on which vehicles can run throughout the year).

d) **Golden Quadrilateral Project**: It includes 5,846 Km long 4/6 lane high density traffic corridors which connect the four big metropolises of the country - Delhi, Mumbai, Chennai and Kolkata. With the construction of Golden Quadrilateral, the distance and time between these metropolises of India and the cost of transportation mainly reduced.

e) North-South and East-West Corridors **(Super Corridors)**: The objective of the North-South Corridor is to connect Srinagar in Jammu and Kashmir to Kanyakumari in Tamil Nadu through a 4,016 Km long route. The objective of the East and West Corridor is to connect Silchar in Assam to Porbandar in Gujarat through a 3,640 Km long route.

5. **In how many forms have roads been classified for the purpose of construction and maintenance?.**

   After independence, a twenty-year road plan (1961) was started to improve the condition of roads in India, in which roads were classified for the purpose of construction and maintenance as follows--

   A. National Highways-

   a) Those major roads, which are constructed and maintained by the Central Government, are known as National Highways.

   b) These roads are used for inter-state transportation and movement of defense material and army to strategic areas.

c) These highways connect the state capitals, major cities, important ports and railway junctions.

d) The length of national highways has increased from 19,700 Km in 1951 to 1,01,011 Km in 2016.

e) The length of national highways is only 2% of the total length of roads in the entire country, but they carry 40% of the road traffic.

B. State Highways-

a) These roads are constructed and maintained by the state governments.

b) They connect the state capital to district headquarters and other important cities. These roads are connected to national highways.

c) 4 percent of the total length of roads in the country comes under them.

C. District Roads-

a) These roads serve as connecting roads between district headquarters and other important places in the district.

b) 14% of the total length of roads in the country comes under them.

D. Rural roads-

a) These roads are very important for connecting rural areas.

b) About 80 percent of the total road length in India is classified as rural roads.

c) There is regional disparity in the density of rural roads as they are influenced by the nature of the terrain.

6. Why is the density of rural roads very low in mountainous, plateau and forested areas?

a) About 80 per cent of the total length of roads in India is classified as rural roads.

b) There is regional disparity in the density of rural roads because they are affected by the nature of the terrain. The length of roads per 100 sq. km. area is called road density. Due to population pressure in the Himalayan mountainous region, north-eastern region, Rajasthan etc., road density is found to be low.

c) Road network is found to be less on relatively rough and fragmented terrains. The density of roads is also low in high slope and hilly areas.

d) Road density is found to be low in rural, mountainous and forested areas due to transportation of relatively fewer people, less distance and less goods.

e) In rural areas, unpaved roads become unusable during the rainy season.

7. Mention the role of National Highways Authority of India.

a) National Highways Authority of India (NHAI) became operational in 1995.

b) It is an autonomous body under the Ministry of Surface Transport.

c) It has been entrusted with the responsibility of development, maintenance and operation of national highways.

d) Along with this, it is an apex body for quality improvement of roads designated as national highways.

8. Which apex body develops border roads? Describe the main functions of the institution.

a) Border Roads Organization is the apex body for development of border roads in the country. It was formed in May 1960.

b) This institution works to accelerate economic development and strengthen defense preparedness through rapid and coordinated improvement of strategically important roads along the northern and north-eastern borders of the country.

c) It is a leading multi-faceted construction agency. It has built a road connecting Chandigarh to Manali (Himachal Pradesh) and Leh (Ladakh) in the mountainous regions situated at an average height of 4,270 meters above sea level.

d) BRO not only builds and maintains roads in strategically sensitive areas, but also takes the responsibility of removing snow in high altitude areas.

9. Explain the importance of Border Roads.
  a) Border roads are of strategic importance. These roads provide ration and other facilities to the army in the border areas.
  b) The development of these roads increases accessibility in the inaccessible border areas.
  c) These roads have also proved helpful in the economic development of border areas.
  d) These roads are important for international border security.
  e) These roads connect remote border rural areas to the main and central land.

10. Mention the features of Atal Tunnel.
  a) Atal Tunnel (World's longest highway, 9.02 km) is built by BRO.
  b) This tunnel connects Manali to Lahaul-Spiti valley throughout the year. Earlier this valley remained isolated for about 6 months due to heavy snowfall.
  c) This tunnel is built with ultra-modern facilities at an altitude of 3000 meters above mean sea level in the Pir Panjal range of Himalayas.

11. Objectives of Bharatmala scheme.
  b) Bharatmala is a proposed umbrella scheme.
  c) It focused on the development of State roads along coastal border areas, including connectivity of non major ports.
  d) Its covers Backward areas religious and tourist places connectivity programme.
  e) **Setubharatam Pariyojana**, which is for the consruction of about 1500 major bridges and 200 rail over bridges rail under bridges; District Headquarters connectivity.
  f) This scheme for the development of about 9000 km newly declared National Highways.

12. Explain the purpose of International Highways of India with examples.
  a) The purpose of International Highways is to promote cordial relations between neighboring countries.

b) International Highways providing effective connectivity between attached world and India.

c) Khardung La Pass in Jammu and Kashmir.

d) Delhi-Lahore bus service from Wagah Border.

e) Aman Setu located between Srinagar and Muzaffarabad.

13. **"Indian railway network is one of the longest in the world and has contributed significantly to the economic development of the country." Justify this statement.**

a) According to Mahatma Gandhi, Indian Railways has contributed to India's freedom struggle by bringing together people of diverse cultures.

b) Indian Railways was established in 1853 and a 34 km long railway line was constructed between Mumbai and Thane.

c) The total length of the Indian railway network is 66030 Km. Due to its very large size, Indian Railways has been divided into 18 divisions.

d) Urban areas, raw material/material producing areas, plantations and other commercial crop areas, hill stations and cantonment areas are well connected by railways, due to which the resources could be used properly.

e) After the independence of the country, these railways were also expanded to other areas, such as Konkan Railway which provides direct connectivity between Mumbai and Mangalore along the western sea coast of India.

14. **On the basis of the width of the railway track, Indian Railways has been classified into how many classes?**

    On the basis of the width of the railway track, Indian Railways has been divided into three classes-

A) **Broad Gauge** - In this, the distance between the railway tracks is 1.616 meters. The total length of the broad gauge line is about 60510 Km.

B) **Meter Gauge** - In this, the distance between two railway tracks is one meter. Its total length is about 3880 Km.

C) **Narrow Gauge** - In this, the distance between two railway tracks is 0.762 meters or 0.610 meters. Its total length is about 2297 Km. It is mostly limited to mountainous areas.

15. Explain the importance of Konkan Railway.

a) Konkan Railway, built in 1998, is an important achievement of Indian Railways.

b) The 760 Km long railway line connects Roha in Maharashtra to Mangalore in Karnataka.

c) It is considered a unique marvel of engineering.

d) This railway line crosses 146 rivers, 2000 bridges & 91 tunnels.

e) Asia's longest tunnel of 6.5 Km is also present on this route.

f) Karnataka, Goa and Maharashtra states are partners in this.

16. Explain with examples any five steps taken to increase the efficiency and quality of Indian Railways.

a) Indian Railways has started a comprehensive program to convert meter gauge and narrow gauge railway lines into broad gauge.

b) Apart from this, diesel and electric engines have been installed in place of steam engines and electrification of the railway route has increased the speed of trains as well as their carrying capacity.

c) The environment of railway stations has also improved due to the replacement of coal-powered steam engines.

d) The process of making the railway crossing free has given impetus to rail traffic.

e) Metro rail has revolutionised urban transport in cities like Kolkata and Delhi.

f) The replacement of diesel-powered buses with CNG-powered vehicles as well as the operation of metro rail is an important step towards controlling air pollution in urban centres.

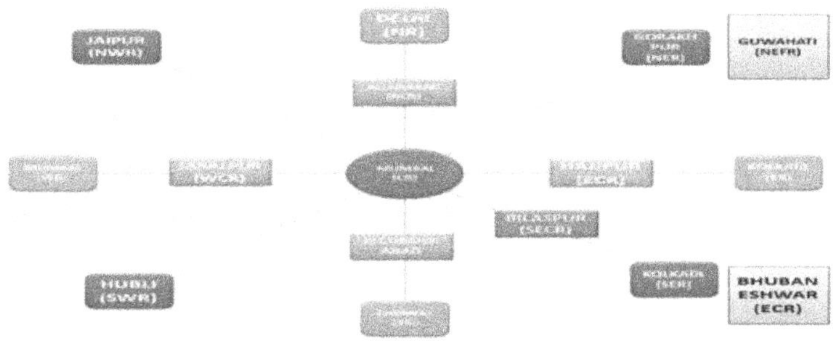

17. **"Waterways in India are an important mode of transport for both passenger and cargo transportation." Justify the statement with examples.**

   a) Water is the cheapest mode of transport and is most suitable for transporting heavy and bulky materials.

   b) It is a fuel-efficient and eco-friendly transport system.

   c) Water transport is of two types – (a) Inland waterways and (b) Oceanic waterways.

   d) In India, about 95% of foreign trade by weight and 70% by value is carried out through oceanic routes.

   e) Water transport routes are mainly used for transport between the mainland and islands of the country.

   f) The backwater routes of Kerala also attract a large number of tourists.

18. **Mention the major problems in the development of inland waterways in India.**

   a) Before the advent of roads and railways, inland waterways were the main mode of transport, but it had to face tough competition with rail and road transport.

   b) Due to the division of river water for irrigation, most parts of their routes are not suitable for navigation.

   c) The speed of water transport is relatively slow.

   d) At present, 14,500 Km long waterways are available for navigation in India, which contributes only 1% to the country's transportation.

   e) This includes rivers, canals, backwaters and narrow bays etc. At present, 5,685 km of major river waterways are navigable by flat-bottomed commercial ships.

19. **Mention the work done for the development of national waterways in the country.**

   Inland Waterways Authority was established in 1986 for the development, maintenance and regulation of national waterways in the country, by which the following national waterways have been declared -

1) National Waterway-1:

a) The first national waterway of the country is from Allahabad to Haldia.

b) This waterway on the Ganga river is 1,620 Km long.

c) It was announced in 1986.

d) It is one of the most important waterways of India which is navigable by mechanized boats up to Patna and by ordinary boats up to Haridwar.

e) It is divided into three parts for developmental purposes- 1. Haldia-Farakka (560 Km), 2. Farakka-Patna (460 Km), 3. Patna-Allahabad (600 Km)

2) National Waterway-2:

a) It is 891 Km long from Sadiya to Dhubri in the Brahmaputra river.

b) The Brahmaputra river is navigable by steamer up to Dibrugarh (1384 Km) which is used by India and Bangladesh in partnership.

3) National Waterway-3:

a) It is 168 Km long from Kottapuram to Kollam. b) It includes the West Coast Canal (168 Km) along with Champakara (14 Km) and Udyog Mandal (23 Km) canals.

4) National Waterway-4:

a) Its length is 1078 km.

b) It is a special extension of Godavari and Krishna rivers along with Kakinada and Puducherry canal stretch.

5) National Waterway-5:

a) Along the Matai River, Mahanadi's delta channel, Brahmani River and East Coast Canal.

b) Special extension of Brahmani River (588 km.)

6) National Waterway-6:

a) The waterway of Barak River from Lakhimpur (Assam) to Bhanga (Karimganj, Assam) has been declared as National Waterway-6 in the year 2013.

b) This waterway is 121 km long.

20. "The backwaters of Kerala have a special significance among the inland waterways." Explain the statement.

a) They provide a cheap means of backwater transport.

b) They also attract a large number of tourists to Kerala.

c) The famous Nehru Trophy Boat Race (Vallamkali) is held in the backwaters.

21. "Ocean routes play an important role in the transport sector of India's economy." Explain.

a) India has an extensive coastline of about 7,517 Km including islands.

b) 12 major and 185 minor ports provide structural support to these routes.

c) In India, about 95% of foreign trade by weight and 70% by value is carried out through ocean routes.

d) Ocean waterways are more useful for long distance import-export of heavy and bulky materials.

e) Along with international trade, these routes are also used for transportation between the mainland and islands of the country.

22. "Air transport is very necessary for a large country like India." Explain the statement with examples.

a) Air transport is the fastest means of transportation from one place to another. It has reduced the distance by reducing the travel time.

b) It is very necessary for a large country like India because the distances here are very long and the terrain and climatic conditions are very diverse.

c) Air transport in India started in 1911, when air mail was started for a distance of 10 Km from Allahabad to Naini.

d) Air transport provides international and domestic air services.

e) Air transport connects all the continents of the world through its services.

f) Pawan Hans is a helicopter service serving in the mountainous areas and is widely used by tourists in the North-East sector.

23. What is Pawan Hans?

a) Pawan Hans is a helicopter service established in 1985.

b) It serves the mountainous regions connecting the inaccessible areas of the country.

c) It is widely used by tourists in the North-East sector.

d) Pawan Hans also provides helicopter services for the petroleum sector.

24. What are the main objectives of UDAN.

a) UDAN (Ude Desh ka Aam Nagrik) is a first-of-its kind scheme globally, designed to jump- start the regional aviation market.

b) Regional Connectivity Scheme (RCS) -UDAN was conceived by the Ministry of Aviation (MoCA) Govt. of India.

c) It's promote regional connectivity by making fly affordable for the common citizen.

d) The central idea of the scheme is to encourage airlines to operate flights on regional and remote routes through enabling policies and extending incentives.

25. Discuss the contribution of 'Air India' and 'Indian' in the field of air transport in India.

a) Air transport in India began in 1911, when air mail was started for a distance of 10 km from Allahabad to Naini.

b) The Air Authority of India (AAI) is responsible for providing safe, efficient air traffic and aeronautical communication services in the Indian airspace.

c) Air transport in India is managed by "Air India". Air India connects all the continents of the world by providing international and domestic air services for passengers and cargo traffic.

d) By nationalizing the air transport, two corporations - Air India Limited and Indian Airlines were formed in 1953 which provided international and domestic air services respectively.

e) In 2007, Indian Airlines merged with Air India.

26. **Analyse any five points of the importance of 'pipelines' as a mode of transport.**
   a) Pipeline is a very convenient and efficient transport system for transporting petroleum and petroleum products and natural gases and liquids over long distances.
   b) Pipeline is also used to supply water to cities and industries.
   c) Some solid substances can be transported by converting them into slurry or slurry.
   d) Iron ore is transported from Kudremukh to Mangalore Port through pipeline.
   e) No fuel is used in pipeline transport.

27. **Describe the distribution of oil and gas pipelines in India with examples.**
   a) Oil India Limited (OIL), established under the administration of the Ministry of Petroleum and Natural Gas, is engaged in the exploration, production and transportation of crude oil and natural gas. It was incorporated as a company in 1959.
   b) Asia's first 1157Km long cross-country pipeline was constructed by IOL (Indian Oil Corporation Limited) from Naharkatiya oil field in Assam to Barauni oil refinery. It was further extended to Kanpur in 1966.
   c) GAIL (Gas Authority of India Limited) was established in 1984 as a public sector undertaking to transport, process and market natural gas.
   d) The first 1,700 km long Hazira-Vijaypur-Jagadishpur (HVJ) cross country gas pipeline constructed by GAIL connects Mumbai High and Bassein gas fields with various fertilizer, power and industrial complexes in western and northern India.
   e) These gas pipelines accelerated the growth of the Indian gas market. Overall, India's gas infrastructure has expanded more than tenfold to 18,500 km and is likely to soon extend to over 34,000 km as a gas grid linking all gas sources and consumer markets across the country, including the northeastern states.

28. What do you mean by 'communication'?

a) The transmission of facts, information, ideas, messages, feelings and data from one place to another is called communication.

b) Based on scale and quality, modes of communication can be divided into categories such as personal communication system and mass communication system.

c) Letters, telephone, telegram, email, e-commerce, fax and Internet are examples of personal communication system.

d) Radio, television, newspapers, books and magazines, cinema, satellite, public meetings and conferences etc. are the means of mass communication.

29. "Internet is the most effective and modern among all personal communication systems." Explain with examples.

a) Internet is the most effective and modern among all personal communication systems. It is widely used in urban areas.

b) www (world wide web) is also known as Internet. It was invented by- Tim Berners-Lee, Robert Cailliau.

c) It helps the user to directly access the world of knowledge and information through e-mail.

d) It is being used more and more for e-commerce and monetary transactions.

e) Internet is like a huge central storehouse of data including detailed information on various items, hence it is also called 'Information Rajpath'.

f) Through Internet and e-mail, this network provides access to information at a relatively low cost.

30. "Television broadcasting has emerged as a highly effective audio-visual medium in dissemination of information and educating the masses." Justify the statement with suitable examples.

a) Television broadcasting has emerged as a highly effective audio-visual medium in dissemination of information and educating the masses.

b) In the initial period, TV services were limited to the national capital only, where it was started in 1959.

c) After 1972, many other centres were started. In 1976, TV was merged with All India Radio and given a separate identity as Doordarshan (DD).

d) After the commissioning of INSAT 1A, common national programmes were started for the entire network and these have been extended to backward and remote rural areas across the country.

e) Special news bulletins are also broadcast on special occasions like sessions of Parliament and State Legislatures.

31. **What changes has radio brought in the socio-cultural life of people?**

a) Radio broadcasting in India was started in 1923 by the Radio Club of Bombay.

b) Within a short period, it has found a place in every home across the country.

c) The government took control of this popular medium of communication under the Indian Broadcasting System in 1930.

d) In 1936, it was changed to ALL INDIA RADIO (AIR) and in 1957 to Akashvani.

e) All India Radio broadcasts various types of programs related to information, education and entertainment.

f) Special news bulletins are also broadcast through television on special occasions such as during the sessions of Parliament and State Assemblies.

32. **"Satellites are a mode of communication in themselves and they also regulate other means of communication." Analyze the statement.**

a) Satellite communication has become important for economic and strategic reasons.

b) We get a wide view of the area by using satellite.

c) The images obtained from the satellite can be used for weather forecasting, monitoring natural disasters, surveillance of border areas etc.

d) Satellite communication provided servives to telephone companies, as well as wireless, mobile network providers.

e) Information can be exchanged over long distances in any weather and situation through satellite communication.

f) Satellite communications use solar power which conserves energy and reduces dependence on power-based communication system.

33. Give a brief account on India's satellite system.

a) India's satellite system can be classified into two parts on the basis of configuration and objectives - Indian National Satellite System (INSAT) and Indian Remote Sensing Satellite (IRS-Indian Remote Sensing) System.

b) INSAT was established in 1983. It is a multipurpose satellite system which is useful for telecommunication, meteorological observations and various other data and programs.

c) I.R.S. satellite system was started in March 1988 with the cooperation of Russia. India also developed its own launch vehicle PSLV (Polar Satellite Launch Vehicle).

d) National Remote Sensing Centre (NRSC) located at Hyderabad provides facilities for acquisition and processing of data.

e) These satellites collect data in various spectral bands and transmit it to ground stations for various uses. These are very useful for management of natural resources.

<u>Objectives</u>

1) Who said "Indian Railways has contributed to India's freedom struggle by bringing together people of diverse cultures.
   a) Bal Gangadhar Tilak   b) Rabindranath Tagore
   c) J.L. Nehru   d) M.K. Gandhi

2) The first serious attempt plan at road development was
   a) Raipur Plan   b) Kanpur Plan

    c) Nagpur Plan   d) Udaipur Plan

3) Which of the following is not a correct match?
    a) South Eastern - Kolkata   b) South East Central - Raipur
    c) West Central - Jabalpur   d) East Central - Hajipur

4) National Waterway No. 1 between which two places?
    a) Sadiya - Dhubri   b) Haldia - Allahabad
    c) Silchar - Karimganj   d) Kolkata - Farakka

5) In which of the following years was the first radio program broadcast?
    a) 1911   b) 1927
    c) 1936   d) 1923

6) Atal Tunnel connects which of the following?
    a) Manali to Leh-Ladakh   b) Manali to Spiti Valley
    c) Sikkim to Tibet   d) Guwahati to Tawang

7) Setu Bharatam Project is related to which mode of transport?
    a) Road   b) Rail
    c) Air service   d) Water transport

8) Which of the following is not a correct match?
    a) 20 Year Road Plan – 1961
    b) National Highway Authority of India (NHAI) – 1955
    c) Border Roads Organisation (BRO) – 1965
    d) Inland Waterways Authority – 1986

9) Arrange the following in decreasing order of their total length-
    a) National Highway, State Highway, District Roads, Rural Roads
    b) State Highway, National Highway, Rural Roads, District Roads
    c) District Roads, Rural Roads, National Highway, State Highway
    d) Rural Roads, District Roads, State Highway, National Highway

10) The first Indian railway was started from where to where?
    a) Mumbai to Pune   b) Mumbai to Thane
    c) Mumbai to Nagpur   d) Mumbai to Surat

11) Where is the Konkan Railway from?
    a) Amroha to Kanpur   b) Bangalore to Mangalore
    c) Roha to Mangalore   d) Mumbai to Vasco da Gama

12) Where is the National Remote Sensing Centre (NRSC) located?
    a) Dehradun   b) Sriharikota

c) Ahmedabad   d) Hyderabad

13) Which cities located on the northern and eastern ends of the Golden Quadrilateral project?
a) Delhi and Mumbai   b) Delhi and Kolkata
c) Srinagar and Kanyakumari   d) Porbandar and Silchar

14) India's road network holds what position in the world?
a) First   b) Second
c) Third   d) Fourth

15) Waterways in India contribute how much percent to the total transportation of the country?
a) 1%   b) 10%
c) 15%   d) 20%

16) Study the following table carefully and answer the question that follow:

India Road Network 2020

Sr. No.	Road Category	Length in Km
1	National Highways	136440
2	State Highways	176818
3	Others	5902539
	Total	6215797

National highways are less by how many km with respect to state highways in 2020?
a) 40,378   b) 5,766,099
c) 6,079,357   d) 50,000

17) Which one of the following is not correctly matched?

a) Bharatmala Scheme	Development of State roads along coastal border areas.
b) Setubharatam Pariyojana	Development of minor sea ports in India.
c) UDAN ((Ude Desh ka Aam Nagrik)	Promote regional connectivity by making fly affordable for the common citizen.
d) Atal Tunnel	The World's longest highway tunnel.

Answers: 1-d, 2-c, 3-b, 4-b, 5-d, 6-b, 7-a, 8-c, 9-d, 10-b, 11-c, 12-d, 13-b, 14-b, 15-a, 16-a, 17-b

CHAPTER 8 – INTERNATIONAL TRADE

1) Examine the changing pattern of India's international trade.

a) India has an important role in the world economy.

b) India's share in world trade is only 1% of the total volume.

c) The value of India's foreign trade was Rs. 1,214 crore in the year 1950-51, which increased to Rs. 44,29,762 crore in the year 2016-17.

d) There are many reasons for this rapid growth in foreign trade such as momentum in the manufacturing sector, liberal policies of the government and diversification of markets etc.

e) There has been a change in the nature of India's foreign trade.

f) The volume of both imports and exports in the country has increased, but the value of imports is higher than exports.

2) Discuss the changing pattern of India's export composition.

a) The composition of goods in India's international trade has changed over time.

b) The share of agriculture and allied products has decreased, while petroleum and crude products and other commodities have increased.

c) The share of ore minerals and manufactured goods has remained broadly stable from 2009-10 to 2010-11 and from 2015-16 to 2016-17.

d) The main reason for the decline in trade of traditional commodities is stiff international competition.

e) Under agricultural products, exports of traditional commodities like coffee, cashew, pulses, etc. have declined.

f) However, exports of floriculture products, fresh fruits, marine products and sugar, etc. have increased.

g) During the year 2016-17, the manufacturing sector alone recorded a share of 73.6% in India's total export value.

h) China and other East Asian countries are major competitors.

i) Gems and jewellery have a major share in India's foreign trade.

3. **What is Hinterland?**

   a) The hinterland is the area of influence of a port which is well connected to the port by rail and road.

   b) Products of this area are sent to the port for export and imported goods are distributed here for sale/consumption.

   c) It is difficult to demarcate the boundaries of the hinterland because it is not fixed in area.

   d) Mostly the hinterland of one port is connected to the hinterland of another port.

4. **Discuss the changing pattern of import composition of India.**

   a) Due to severe shortage of food grains in the 1950s and 1960s, the major items of import in India were food grains, capital goods, machinery and equipment etc.

   b) After the 1970s, due to the success of the Green Revolution, the import of food grains decreased but due to the energy crisis of 1973, the import of petroleum (products) and fertilizers became prominent.

   c) Machinery and equipment, steel, edible oils and chemicals constitute the major import trade. There has been a sharp increase in the import of petroleum and its products.

   d) Petroleum is not only used as fuel but also as raw material in industries. This indicates growing industrialization and better living standards.

   e) There has been a steady increase in the import of capital goods due to the increasing demand from export-oriented industries and the domestic sector. Non-electrical machinery, transport equipment, metal manufactures and machine tools etc. were the main items of capital goods.

   f) There has been a decline in the import of food and allied products along with edible oils.

   g) Other major items of India's imports include pearls, semiprecious stones, gold and silver, metallic ores, and metal scraps, non-ferrous metals and electronic goods etc.

5. Mention the direction of India's international trade.

a) India has trade relations with most countries and major trading groups of the world. During the year 2016-17.

b) The highest international trade, region-wise and sub-region-wise, was with the continental Asian countries.

c) India aims to double its share in international trade during the next five years.

d) For this, favourable measures have been taken like import liberalisation, reduction in import duties, de-licensing and change of patent from process to product.

e) India's foreign trade is mostly conducted through sea & air routes.

f) A small part of foreign trade is done by road in neighbouring states like Nepal, Bhutan, Bangladesh and Pakistan.

6. Seaports called the gateways of international trade? Explain.

a) India is surrounded by sea on three sides with a long coastline.

b) Water provides a flat surface for cheap transportation.

c) Sea travel has a long tradition in India, many places have the nickname port attached to them. Example- Visakhapatnam.

d) There are 12 major and 200 minor or medium ports in India. Some ports have a wide sphere of influence while some have a limited sphere of influence.

e) The central government makes policies and performs regulatory functions in respect of major ports.

f) State governments make policies and perform regulatory functions for minor ports.

g) Major ports handle a large share of the total traffic. The British used these ports as centres of absorption of the resources of their hinterland.

h) The expansion of railways in the hinterland facilitated the linking of local markets with regional markets and regional markets with national markets and national markets with international markets.

7. Explain the development of ports in India after independence.

a) The partition of the country led to the loss of two of India's most important ports, Karachi port to Pakistan and Chittagong port to Bangladesh (then East Pakistan). In spite of this great loss, Indian ports have been growing steadily since the country attained independence.

b) To compensate, several new ports were developed such as Kandla in the west and Diamond Harbour near Kolkata on the Hooghly river in the east.

c) Today Indian ports are handling a large volume of domestic as well as foreign trade. Most of the ports are equipped with modern infrastructure.

d) Earlier the responsibility of development and modernization of ports was on government agencies, but the increased workload and the need to bring these ports at par with international ports invited private entrepreneurs to modernize India's ports.

e) Today the cargo handling capacity of Indian ports has increased from 20 million tonnes in 1951 to over 837 million tonnes in 2016.

8. What are the major ports on the west coast of India?

1. Kandla-

a) Located at the mouth of the Gulf of Kutch, it caters to the western and north-western parts.

b) It is developed to reduce pressure on Mumbai Port.

c) This port is specially designed to receive large volumes of petroleum, petroleum products and fertilizers.

d) An offshore terminal has been developed at Vadinar to reduce pressure on Kandla Port.

2. Mumbai

a) It is a natural port and the largest port of the country.

b) This port is located near the common route of the Middle East, Mediterranean countries, North Africa, North America and European countries from where most of the foreign trade of the country is conducted.

c) 20 Km long and 6-10 Km wide, this port is the largest terminal of the country. Parts of Madhya Pradesh, Maharashtra, Gujarat, Uttar Pradesh and Rajasthan form the backdrop of Mumbai Port.

d) Jawaharlal Nehru Port was developed as a subsidiary port to reduce the pressure of Mumbai Port at Nhava-Sheva. It is the largest container port of India.

3. Marmagao Port

a) It is a natural port of Goa located at the mouth of Zuari River.

b) Iron ore is exported to Japan from here.

c) Konkan Railway has made significant expansion in the hinterland of this port.

d) Karnataka, Goa and Southern Maharashtra form its backdrop.

4. New Mangalore Port

a) This is located in Karnataka and caters to the export requirement of iron ore.

b) This port handles fertilizers, petroleum products, edible oils, coffee, tea, pulp, cotton, molasses, granite stone, etc.

c) Karnataka is the main hinterland of this port.

5. Kochi Port

a) Kochi is a natural port situated at mouth of Bevanad Kayal.

b) This port has the advantage of being located near the Suez Colombo route.

c) It caters to the requirements of Kerala, Southern Karnataka and South Western Tamil Nadu.

9. Which are the major ports located on east coast of India?

1. Kolkata Port

a) Situated on the Hooghly River, which is located 128 km inside the Bay of Bengal.

b) Its hinterland includes Uttar Pradesh, Bihar, Jharkhand, West Bengal and the north-eastern states.

c) This port provides facilities to landlocked neighbouring countries like Bhutan and Nepal.

2. Haldia Port

a) Situated 105 km down stream from Kolkata.

b) It is constructed to reduce the congestion of Kolkata Port.

c) It handles bulk cargo such as iron ore, coal, petroleum products, fertilizers, jute products, cotton & cotton yarn etc.

3. Paradip Port

a) Situated on the Mahanadi delta, 100 km from Cuttack.

b) It is the deepest port.

c) It is developed mainly for export of iron ore on a large scale.

d) The hinterland includes Odisha, Jharkhand & Chhattisgarh.

4. Visakhapatnam Port

a) It is a **landlocked** port located in Andhra Pradesh, it is connected to the sea by a canal through solid rocks & sand.

b) The port has been developed for the disposal of iron ore, petroleum and cargo.

c) The main hinterland is Andhra Pradesh and Telangana.

5. Chennai Port

a) It is one of the oldest ports located on the east coast.

b) It is an artificial port which was built in 1859.

c) The port is not suitable for large ships due to shallow water near the coast.

d) Tamil Nadu and Puducherry are its hinterland.

6. Ennore Port

a) It is built to reduce pressure on Chennai Port on it's north.

7. Tuticorin Port

a) This was also developed to reduce pressure on Chennai Port.

b) Products like coal, salt, food grains, edible oil, sugar, chemicals and petroleum are handled here.

<u>Objectives</u>

1) Which one of the following is a landlocked port?
   a) Visakhapatnam   b) Kandla
   c) Mumbai   d) Haldia

2) Most of India's foreign trade is carried-
   a) By land and sea
   b) By land and air
   c) By sea and air
   d) By sea only

3) Which port was developed to compensate for the loss of Chittagong port due to partition?
   a) Kandla
   b) Haldia
   c) Diamond Harbour
   d) Paradip

4) Rapid increase in import of which of the following goods indicates rising industrialization and better standard of living?
   a) Gold and silver
   b) Textiles
   c) Edible oil
   d) Petroleum

5) Statement I: There has been an increase in the volume of both imports and exports in the country.
   Statement II: In India's foreign trade, the value of exports is higher than that of imports.
   a) Statement I is true but Statement II is false
   b) Statement I is false but Statement II is true.
   c) Both is true
   d) Boath are false

6) Which is popularly known as 'Queen of Arabian Sea'?
   a) Kochi Port
   b) Vembanad Kayal
   c) Pulicat Lake
   d) Chilika Lake

7) India's import composition is highest from which continent?
   a) Europe
   b) Asia/
   c) N America
   d) Africa

8) What measures India will take to double its share in international trade?
   a) Import liberalization
   b) reduction in import duties
   c) delicensing
   d) All

9) The main share of India's exports is?
   a) Fuel
   b) Manufactured goods
   c) Food products
   d) Capital goods

10) Which of the following ports is not a natural port?
    a) Chennai
    b) Mumbai
    c) Marmagao
    d) Kochi

Answers: 1-a, 2-c, 3-c, 4-d, 5-a, 6-b, 7-b, 8-d, 9-b, 10-a

CHAPTER 9 - GEOGRAPHICAL PERSPECTIVE ON SELECTED ISSUES AND PROBLEMS

1) What is the difference between pollution and pollutants?

a) Accumulation of unwanted substances and energy in the environment as a result of human activities is called pollution.

b) On the basis of transport and diffusion of pollutants, pollution is of the following types- water, air, noise and land pollution.

c) Pollutants are those physical, chemical or biological substances which are inadvertently released into the environment and are directly or indirectly harmful to human society and other living beings.

d) Pollutants are such substances due to which pollution spreads in the environment. Such as garbage (waste), lead, ash, carbon dioxide, oxides of nitrogen and sulphur dioxide, chemical fertilizers and pesticides, electric residues, e-waste etc.

2. Describe the nature of water pollution in India.

a) Due to increasing population and industrial expansion, the quality of water has decreased due to indiscriminate use of water.

b) Due to the concentration of organic and inorganic substances in water, the self-purification capacity is not able to purify the water.

c) Water gets contaminated due to dead bodies, decaying animal and plant remains.

d) Industrial waste, poisonous chemicals etc. dissolve in water.

e) Underground water and rivers are also affected by pesticides, fertilizers etc. used in agriculture.

f) Religious-cultural activities are also the cause of water pollution.

g) Contaminated water causes many diseases like diarrhea.

3. What are the main sources and effects of air pollution?
Source-

a) Air pollution spreads due to the emission of toxic smoke gases due to the use of different types of fuels.
b) Burning of fuel, mining, and industries are the main sources of air pollution.
c) These processes release pollutants like sulfur, nitrogen, lead and asbestos in the air.

Effects-

a) Respiratory system, nervous system and blood circulation related diseases occur.
b) **Acid rain** in cities is caused by air pollution.
c) The fog above cities combines with smoke to form **smog** which harms the environment.

4. **What are the main sources and effects of noise pollution?**

a) Noise pollution is when the sound produced from various sources is beyond the human tolerable limit & uncomfortable.
b) **Source-** Noise from industries such as cutting and crushing of stones, heating and beating of steel (blacksmith work), loudspeakers, vendors shouting to sell their goods, movement of heavy transport vehicles, trains and airplanes etc. produce annoying sounds.
c) **Effect-** The loudness of sound is measured in decibels (dB).
   1. There are many sources of noise pollution both inside and outside the house.
   2. Noise pollution causes the most discomfort and irritation. It disrupts sleep, can cause hypertension, emotional problems such as anger, depression and irritability.
   3. Noise pollution has an adverse effect on a person's efficiency and capacity.
d) **Prevention-**
   1) Measures to reduce noise include construction of noise mounds, construction of sound attenuating walls.
   2) Need to install sound barriers and implement noise rules.
   3) Green belts of dense trees help in reducing noise pollution.
   4) Increasing human awareness.

5. What are the main problems associated with urban waste disposal?

   a) Solid waste includes rusted pins, broken glass, plastic, polythene, electrical items, faeces and urine etc. found at different places.

   b) These are disposed of on domestic and commercial basis.

   c) The unpleasant smell of solid waste, flies & dead tissues cause diseases like typhoid, diphtheria, diarrhoea & cholera etc.

   d) Methane gas starts forming when untreated waste rots.

   e) It is not disposed of properly except in metro cities.

   f) Waste should be treated and used for energy production and composting.

6. How is Daurala an exemplary example of ecological recharge and protection of human health? Explain.

   a) Daurala is a village in Meerut whose ground water was highly polluted due to accumulation of heavy metals due to untreated waste water from industries.

   b) NGOs, rural community and public representatives together tried to find a sustainable solution to the problem.

   c) Potable water was made available by increasing the capacity of the Over Head Tank.

   d) The pond was cleaned and renovated.

   e) A structure for rainwater harvesting was built.

   f) 1000 trees were planted.

7. What is a slum settlement? What are the main problems of slum settlements?

   a) Slum settlements are the least desirable residential areas.

   b) Dharavi (Mumbai) is the largest slum settlement in Asia.

   c) It has dilapidated houses.

   d) The following health facilities are found.

   e) There is a lack of drinking water, proper lighting and open air.

   f) Open defecation, irregular drainage.

   g) Crowded roads.

h) There are illegal activities and other social problems due to which diseases like AIDS spread.

i) These settlements are made up of workers engaged in the unorganized sector who are unable to live a better life due to low income.

j) Many diseases spread due to infection caused by pollution.

8. How Jhabua (MP) district presents an example for reducing land degradation.

a) Soil erosion, excessive waterlogging and soil salinity cause land degradation.

b) Jhabua district of Madhya Pradesh is among the 5 most backward districts of the country.

c) It is the inhabited area of Bhil tribe.

d) Water supply management program and collective participation have improved the livelihood of the people.

e) By the community using common property resources.

f) Every family planted a tree and protected it.

g) By developing pastures.

h) Mutual disputes were resolved together.

9. What are the main features of the Namami Gange programme?

a) Ganga as a river has national importance, but there is a need to clean the entire course of the river by controlling pollution. The central government has launched the 'Namami Gange' programme with the following objectives-

b) Providing sewer treatment facilities in cities.

c) Monitoring industrial effluents and developing rivers.

d) Afforestation on the banks of the river to increase biodiversity.

e) Cleaning of river beds.

f) Developing **'Ganga Gram'** in Uttarakhand, Uttar Pradesh, Bihar, Jharkhand.

g) Not throwing any kind of substances into the river, even if they are related to some ritual. This promotes pollution.

h) Creating public awareness.

10. What is the main objective of Swachh Bharat Mission?

a) Swachh Bharat Mission is a part of urban renewal which has been started by the Government of India to improve the quality of life in urban slums.

b) Swachh Bharat Abhiyan is a national level campaign aimed at keeping streets, roads and infrastructure clean and garbage free.

c) The Prime Minister of India launched the Swachh Bharat Mission on 2 October 2014 to achieve universal sanitation.

d) Under the mission, rural India has been declared "Open Defecation Free" (ODF) by building more than 100 million toilets in it.

e) It will be ensured that solid and liquid waste management facilities are available.

<u>Objectives</u>

1) Which tribe is mainly inhabited in Jhabua district?
   a) Gond   b) Santhal
   c) Bhil   d) Gaddi

2) Which of the following is the most polluted river?
   a) Brahmaputra   b) Yamuna
   c) Sutlej   d) Godavari

3) Which of the following disease is water borne?
   a) Conjunctivitis   b) Respiratory infection
   c) Diarrhoea   d) Bronchiolitis

4) Which of the following is a cause of acid rain?
   a) Water pollution   b) Noise pollution
   c) Soil pollution   d) Air pollution

5) Which of the following is the most important cause of water pollution?
   a) Agricultural activity   b) Cultural activity
   c) Industry   d) Domestic waste

6) Which of the following is the most water polluting industry?
   a) Leather industry   b) Plastic industry
   c) Sugar industry   d) Cottage industry

7) The level of constant noise is measured by sound level in____?

    a) Joule   b) Intensity

    c) Decibel   d) Hertz

8) Watershed Management Programme implemented in Jhabua by?

    a) Rural Development   b) Agriculture Ministry

    c) Both a and b   d) Tribal Ministry

9) What is the smoky fog over cities called?

    a) Acid rain   b) Heat island

    c) Smog   d) Smog-fog

10) Which one is not a characteristic of Slums?

    a) Dilapidated houses   b) Individual security

    c) Unregulated drainage   d) Poor ventilation

11. Which one is not a objective of 'Namami Gange Programme'?

    a) Afforestation along the bank   b) Sewerage treatment

    b) Monitoring of industrial effluents   d) Ganga Grams in Assam

12. Which one is an example of solidwaste?

    a) Kitchen discharged items   b) Polythene bags

    c) Plant leaves and branches   d) Old newspapers

13. Which one is not a cause of water pollution by human activity?

    a) Decomposition of animals   b) Industrial wastes

    c) Inorganic fertilisers   d) Religious fairs

14. Who dominates the rural-urban migration flows?

    a) Male   b) Female

    c) Childrens   d) Elderly peoples

15. The Swachh Bharat Mission (SBM) is part of the __________ ?

    a) Watershed Management   b) Namami Gange Programme

    c) Urban renewal mission   d) Bharatmala Priyojna

Answers: 1-c, 2-b, 3-c, 4-d, 5-c, 6-a, 7-c, 8-c, 9-c, 10-b, 11-d, 12-b, 13-a, 14-a, 15-c

MAP

Map Items for identification only on outline political map of the World
Fundamentals of Human Geography (05 Marks)

Chapter No. and Name	Map Items
1 - Human Geography	Nil
2 -The World Population Density Distribution & Growth	Nil
3 - Human Development	Nil
4 - Primary Activities	Areas of subsistence gathering (Fig 4.2) Major areas of nomadic herding of the world (4.4) Major areas of commercial livestock rearing (4.6) Major areas of extensive commercial grain faming (4.12) Major areas of mixed farming of the World (4.14)
5 - Secondary Activities	Nil
6 - Tertiary and Quaternary Activities	Nil
7 - Transport, Communication and Trade	**Terminal Stations of Transcontinental Railways–** Trans-Siberian, Trans Canadian, Trans-Australian Railways **Major Sea Ports** **Europe**: North Cape, London, Hamburg **North America**: Vancouver, San Francisco, New Orleans **South America**: Rio De Janeiro, Colon, Valparaiso **Africa**: Suez and Cape Town **Asia**: Yokohama, Shanghai, Hong Kong, Aden, Karachi, Kolkata **Australia**: Perth, Sydney, Melbourne **Major Airports:** **Asia**: Tokyo, Beijing, Mumbai, Jeddah, Aden **Africa**: Johannesburg & Nairobi **Europe**: Moscow, London, Paris, Berlin and Rome **North America**: Chicago, New Orleans, Mexico City **South America**: Buenos Aires, Santiago **Australia**: Darwin and Wellington **Inland Waterways** Suez Canal, Panama Canal, Rhine waterways & St. Lawrence Seaways
8-International Trade	Nil

Map Items for locating and labelling on political outline map of India
India - People and Economy (5 Marks)

Chapter No. and Name	Map Items
1-Population Distribution Density Growth & Comp.	State with highest & lowest population density (2011)
2-Human Settlement	Nil
3-Land Resources and Agriculture	Leading producing states of the following crops: (a) Rice (b) Wheat (c) Cotton (d) Jute (e) Sugarcane (f) Tea and (g) Coffee
4-Water Resources	Nil
5-Mineral And Energy Resources	**Mines:** • **Iron-ore mines**: Mayurbhanj, Bailadila, Ratnagiri, Bellary • **Manganese mines**: Balaghat, Shimoga • **Copper mines**: Hazaribagh, Singhbhum, Khetari • **Bauxite mines**: Katni, Bilaspur and Koraput • **Coal mines**: Jharia, Bokaro, Raniganj, Neyveli • **Oil Refineries**: Mathura, Jamnager, Barauni
6-Planning and Sustainable Development in Indian Context	Nil
7-Transport and Communication	Nil
8-International Trade (Mark and label the major sea ports and airports on an outline map of India.)	• **Major Sea Ports**: Kandla, Mumbai, Marmagao, Kochi, Mangalore, Tuticorin, Chennai, Vishakhapatnam, Paradwip, Haldia • **International Air ports**: Ahmedabad, Mumbai, Bengaluru, Chennai, Kolkata, Guwahati, Delhi, Amritsar, Thiruvananthapuram & Hyderabad.
9-Geographical Perspective on selected issues & problems	Nil

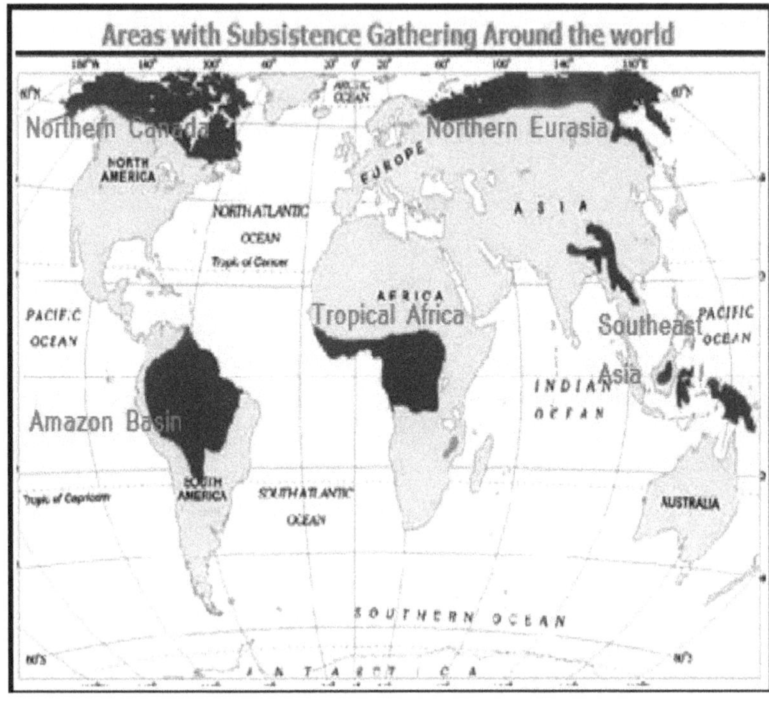

Areas with Subsistence Gathering Around the world
Northern Canada
Northern Eurasia
NORTH AMERICA
EUROPE
ASIA
AFRICA
Tropical Africa
Southeast Asia
Amazon Basin
SOUTH AMERICA
AUSTRALIA
ARCTIC OCEAN
NORTH ATLANTIC OCEAN
Tropic of Cancer
PACIFIC OCEAN
PACIFIC OCEAN
INDIAN OCEAN
Tropic of Capricorn
SOUTH ATLANTIC OCEAN
SOUTHERN OCEAN
ANTARCTICA

Areas of Nomadic Herding around the World
Eurasian Tundra
Mangolia & Middle China
Atlantic coast of North Africa
Arabian Peninsula
South-West Africa
Medagascar Island
NORTH AMERICA
EUROPE
ASIA
AFRICA
SOUTH AMERICA
AUSTRALIA
ARCTIC OCEAN
NORTH ATLANTIC OCEAN
Tropic of Cancer
PACIFIC OCEAN
PACIFIC OCEAN
INDIAN OCEAN
Tropic of Capricorn
SOUTH ATLANTIC OCEAN
SOUTHERN OCEAN
ANTARCTICA

Areas of Commercial Livestock Rearing
ARCTIC OCEAN
60°N
60°N
NORTH AMERICA
EUROPE
Central Asia
Western
ASIA
USA
NORTH ATLANTIC
OCEAN
Tropic of Cancer
PACIFIC OCEAN
PACIFIC OCEAN
AFRICA
INDIAN OCEAN
SOUTH AMERICA
Western Africa
Argentina
& Uruguay
SOUTH ATLANTIC OCEAN
Tropic of Capricorn
Australia
& New
Zealand
SOUTHERN OCEAN
60°S
60°S
ANTARCTICA

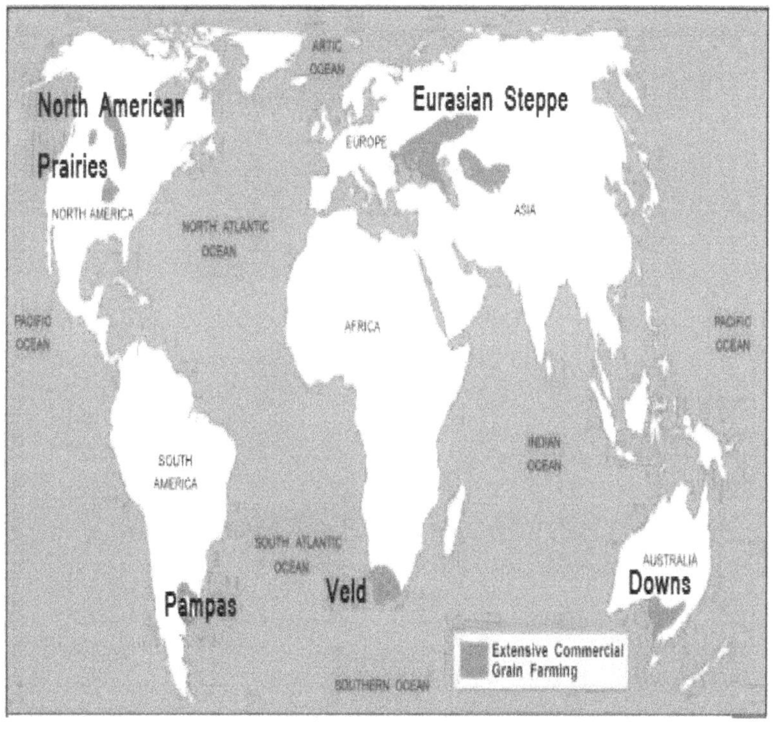

ARTIC OCEAN
North American
Eurasian Steppe
Prairies
EUROPE
NORTH AMERICA
ASIA
NORTH ATLANTIC OCEAN
PACIFIC OCEAN
PACIFIC OCEAN
AFRICA
SOUTH AMERICA
INDIAN OCEAN
SOUTH ATLANTIC OCEAN
AUSTRALIA
Veld
Downs
Pampas
Extensive Commercial Grain Farming
SOUTHERN OCEAN

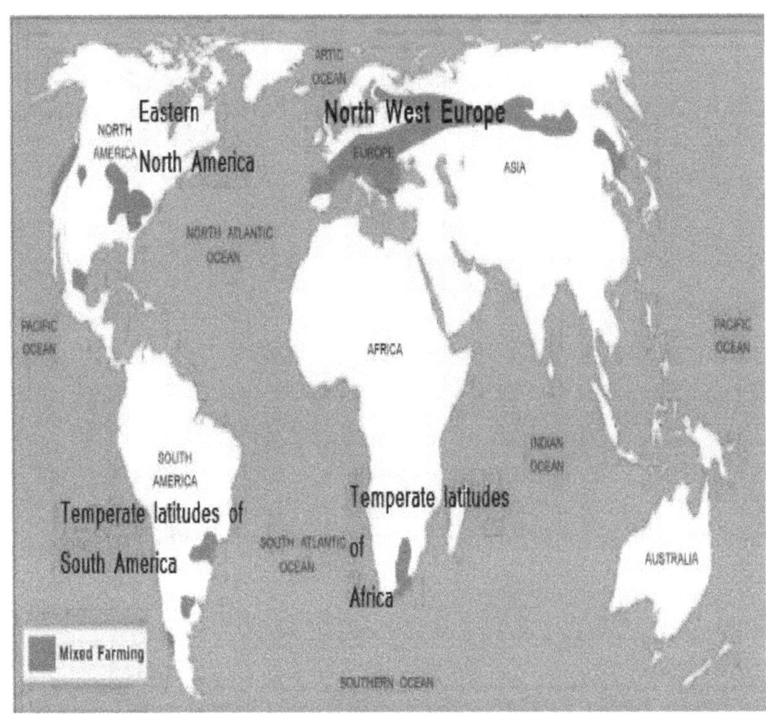

Eastern
North America
North West Europe
NORTH AMERICA
EUROPE
ASIA
NORTH ATLANTIC OCEAN
AFRICA
PACIFIC OCEAN
PACIFIC OCEAN
SOUTH AMERICA
INDIAN OCEAN
Temperate latitudes of South America
SOUTH ATLANTIC OCEAN
Temperate latitudes of Africa
AUSTRALIA
Mixed Farming
SOUTHERN OCEAN

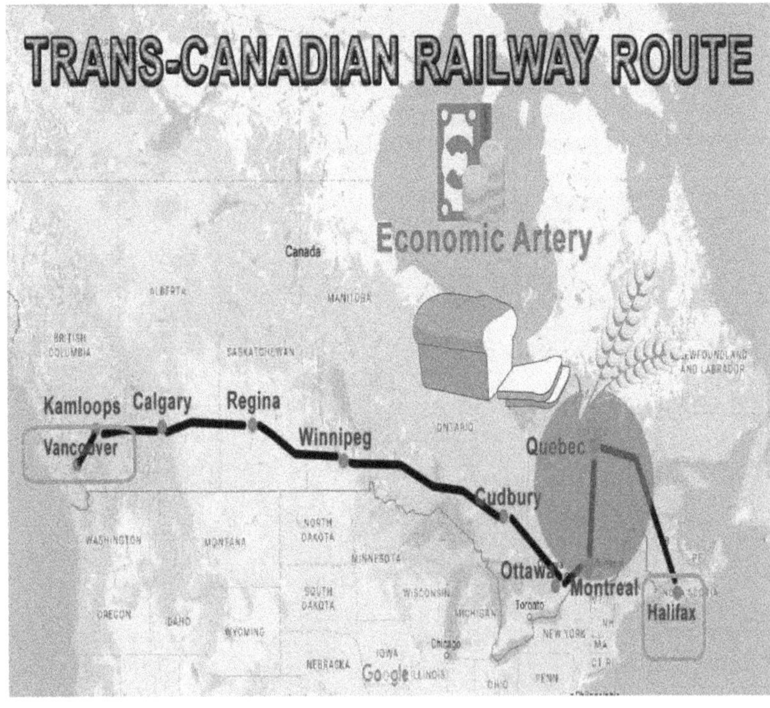

TRANS-CANADIAN RAILWAY ROUTE
Economic Artery
Canada
ALBERTA
MANITOBA
BRITISH COLUMBIA
SASKATCHEWAN
NEWFOUNDLAND AND LABRADOR
Kamloops
Calgary
Regina
Vancouver
Winnipeg
ONTARIO
Quebec
Cudbury
WASHINGTON
MONTANA
NORTH DAKOTA
MINNESOTA
Ottawa
Montreal
OREGON
IDAHO
WYOMING
SOUTH DAKOTA
WISCONSIN
MICHIGAN
Toronto
NEW YORK
Halifax
NEBRASKA
IOWA
Chicago
ILLINOIS
OHIO
PENN
Google

60°W
70°
30°
90°
150°
70°
60°E
ARCTIC
OCEAN
BALTIC SEA
St. Petersburg
50°
SEA
OF
OKHOTSK
50°
Moscow
RUSSIA
Kazan
Yekaterinburg
Tyumen
SOUTH ATLANTIC
OCEAN
Khabarovsk
Omsk
Krasnoyarsk
Novosibirsk
Angarsk
Chita
Vladivostok
CASPIAN SEA
RAILWAY
0   300   600   900 Km
60°
90°
120°E

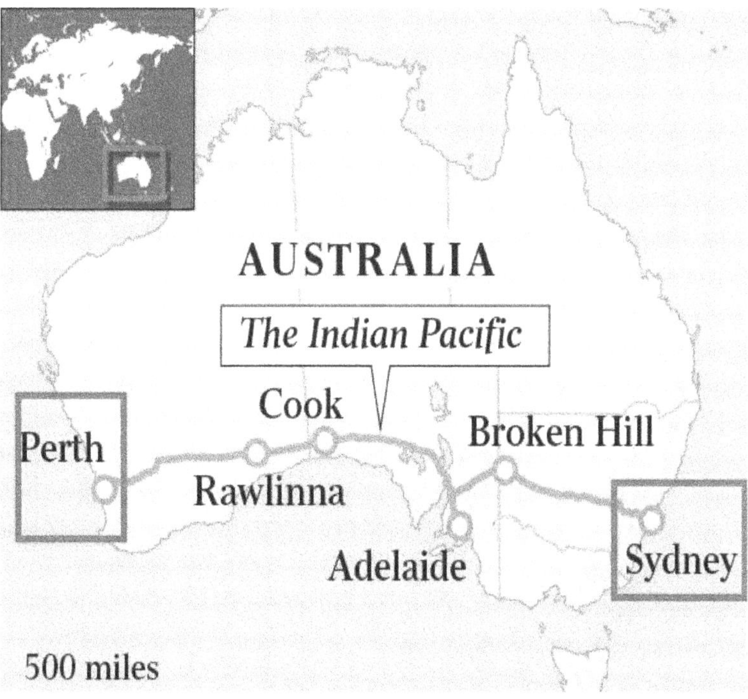

AUSTRALIA
The Indian Pacific
Cook
Broken Hill
Perth
Rawlinna
Adelaide
Sydney
500 miles

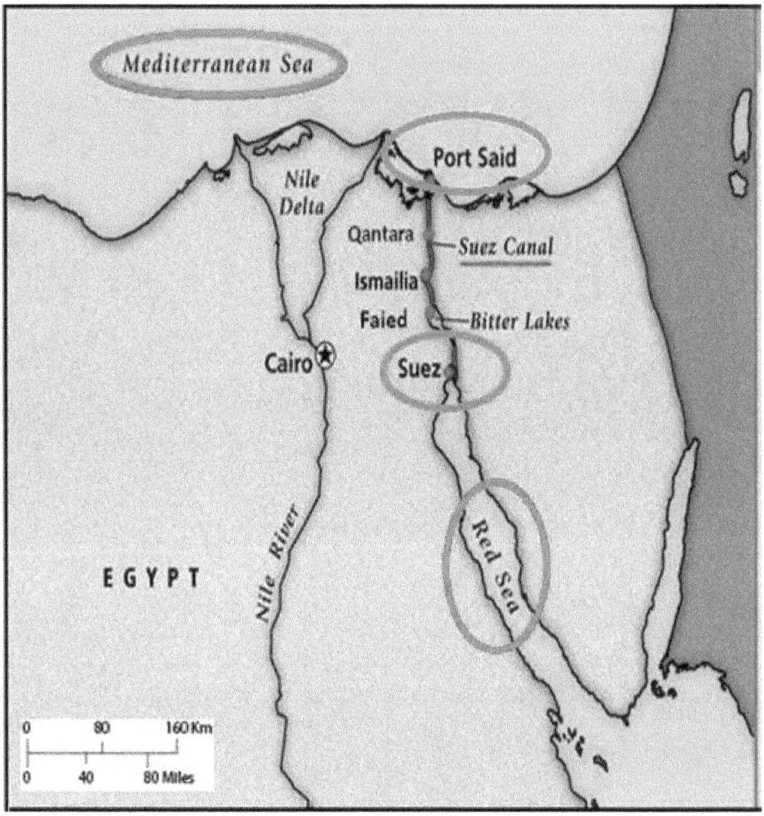

Mediterranean Sea
Port Said
Nile Delta
Qantara
Suez Canal
Ismailia
Faied
Bitter Lakes
Cairo
Suez
Nile River
Red Sea
EGYPT
0   80   160 Km
0   40   80 Miles

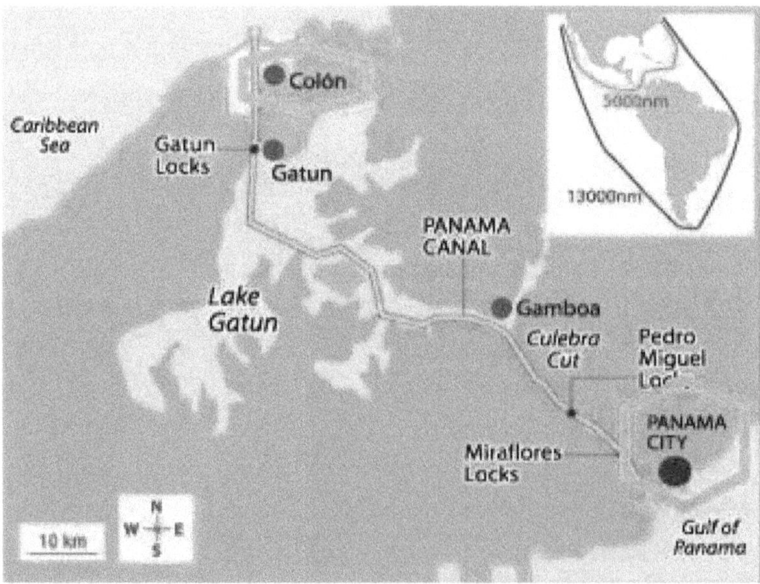

Colón
Caribbean Sea
Gatun Locks
Gatun
PANAMA CANAL
Lake Gatun
Gamboa
Culebra Cut
Pedro Miguel Locks
PANAMA CITY
Miraflores Locks
Gulf of Panama
5000nm
13000nm
N
W
E
S
10 km

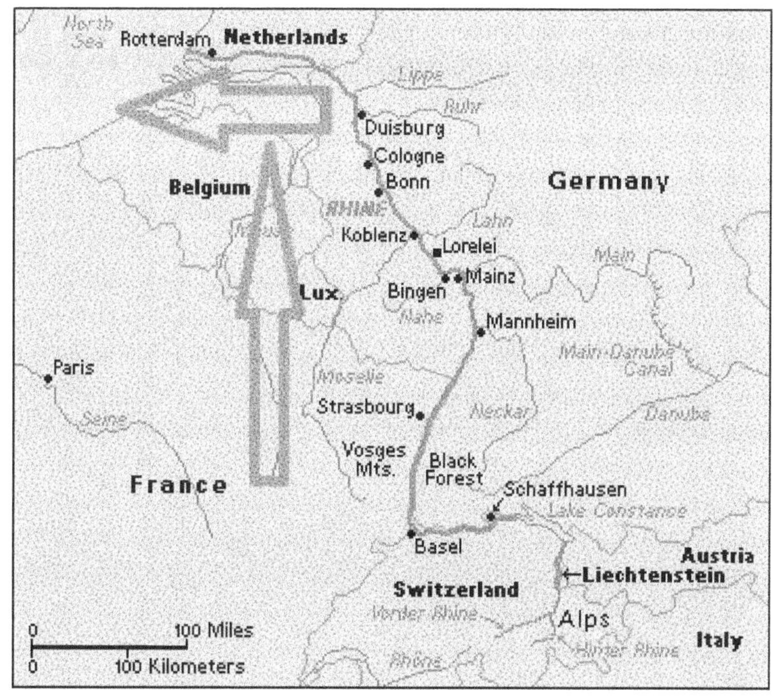
North Sea
Rotterdam
Netherlands
Lippe
Ruhr
Duisburg
Cologne
Bonn
Germany
Belgium
RHINE
Lahn
Koblenz
Lorelei
Main
Mainz
Lux.
Bingen
Nahe
Mannheim
Main-Danube Canal
Meuse
Paris
Seine
Moselle
Strasbourg
Neckar
Danube
Vosges Mts.
Black Forest
Schaffhausen
Lake Constance
France
Basel
Austria
←Liechtenstein
Switzerland
Vorder Rhine
Alps
Italy
Hinter Rhine
Rhine
0   100 Miles
0   100 Kilometers

CANADA
N
W   E
S
Duluth
Lake Superior
Lake Huron
Lake Michigan
Lake Ontario
Lake Erie
Saint Lawrence River
UNITED STATES
ATLANTIC OCEAN

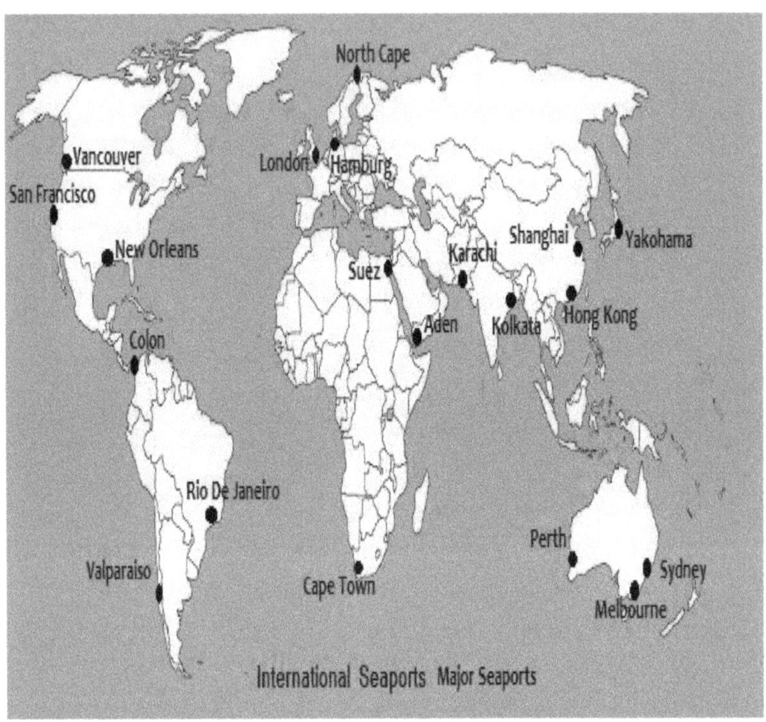
North Cape
Vancouver
London
Hamburg
San Francisco
Shanghai
Yakohama
New Orleans
Karachi
Suez
Aden
Kolkata
Hong Kong
Colon
Rio De Janeiro
Perth
Valparaiso
Cape Town
Sydney
Melbourne
International Seaports Major Seaports

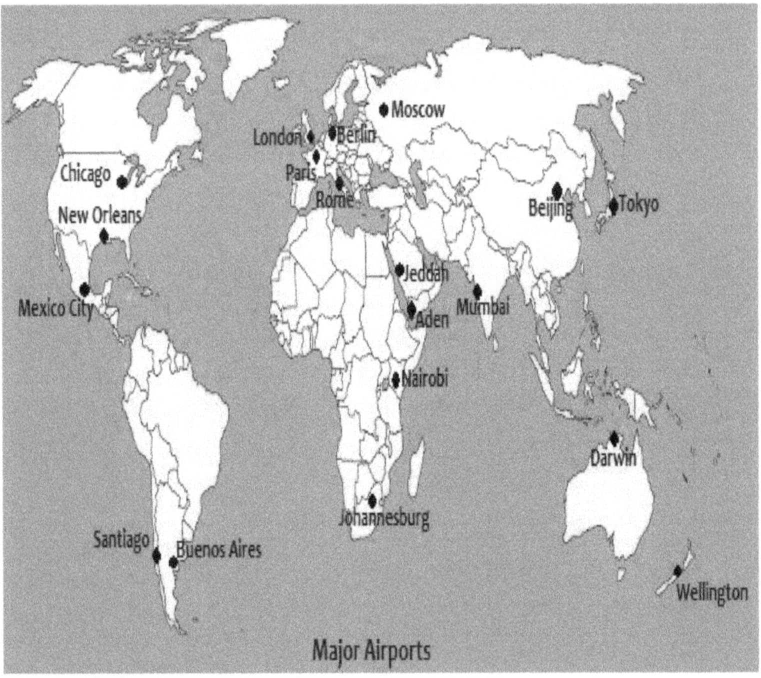
Moscow
London
Berlin
Chicago
Paris
Rome
Beijing
Tokyo
New Orleans
Jeddah
Mumbai
Mexico City
Aden
Nairobi
Darwin
Santiago
Buenos Aires
Johannesburg
Wellington
Major Airports

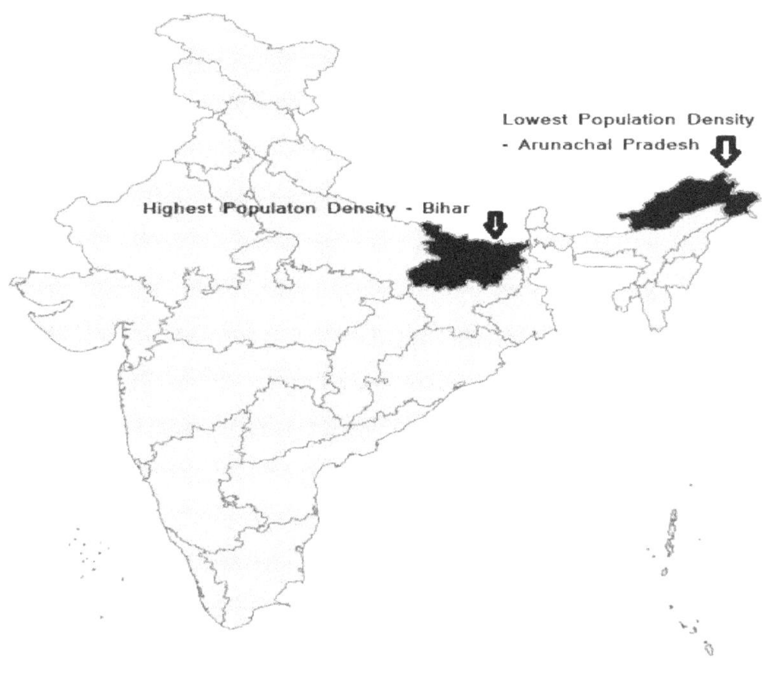

Lowest Population Density - Arunachal Pradesh
Highest Populaton Density - Bihar

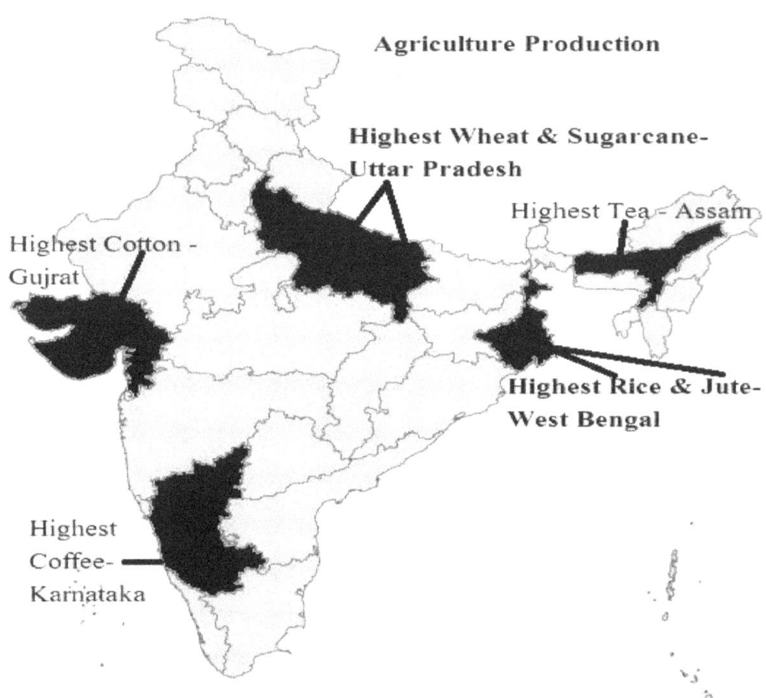

Agriculture Production
Highest Wheat & Sugarcane- Uttar Pradesh
Highest Tea - Assam
Highest Cotton - Gujrat
Highest Rice & Jute- West Bengal
Highest Coffee- Karnataka

Iron Ore
Mayurbhanj
Ratnagiri
Bailadeela
Bellari
MANGANESE MINES
Balaghat
Shimoga

Copper
Khetri
Hazaribag
Singbhumi
BAUXITE MINES
Katni
Bilaspur
Koraput

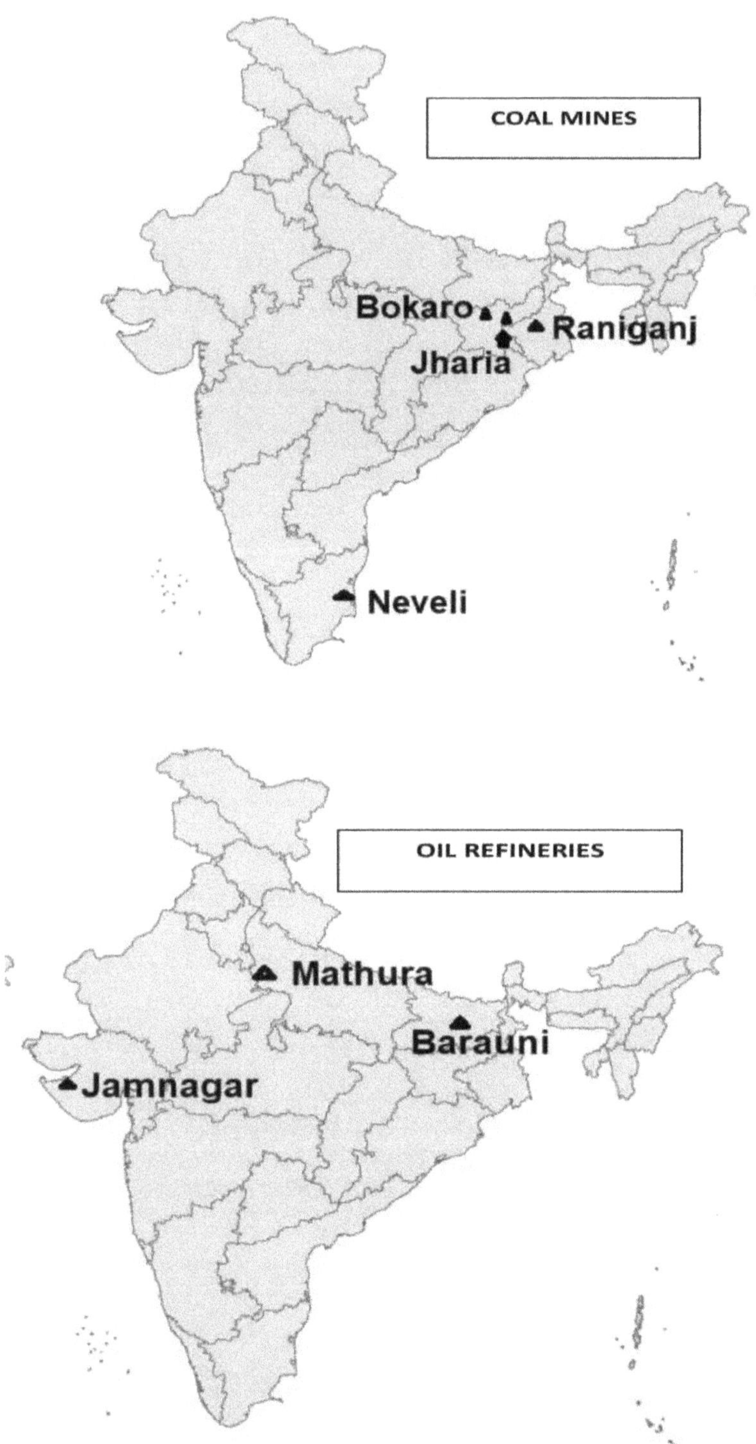
COAL MINES
Bokaro
Jharia
Raniganj
Neveli
OIL REFINERIES
Mathura
Barauni
Jamnagar

INTERNATIONAL AIRPORT
RAJA SANSI INTERNAIONAL AIRPORT
INDIRA GANDHI INTERNATIONAL AIRPORT
GOPINATH BORDOLAI INTERNATIONAL AIRPORT
AHMADABAD INTERNATIONAL AIRPORT
NETAJI SUBASH BOSE INTERNATIONAL AIRPORT
CHHATRAPATI SHIVAJI INTERNATIONAL AIRPORT
RAJIV GANDHI INTERNATIONAL AIRPORT
BANGALURU INTERNATIONAL AIRPORT
MEENAM BAKKAM INTERNATIONAL AIRPORT
THIRUVANANTHAPURAM INTERNATIONAL AIRPORT

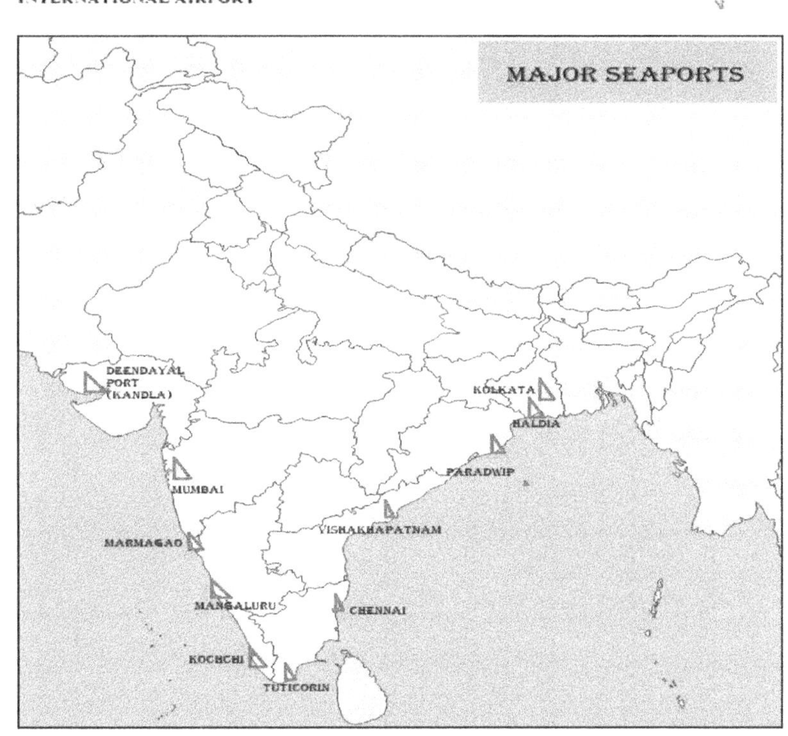
MAJOR SEAPORTS
DEENDAYAL PORT (KANDLA)
KOLKATA
HALDIA
PARADWIP
MUMBAI
VISHAKHAPATNAM
MARMAGAO
MANGALURU
CHENNAI
KOCHCHI
TUTICORIN

Examination Tips

Before the exam

1. Practice all the chapters at least three times.
2. Practice the facts/references given in the box in the book.
3. Try to remember the answer with the help of "Key Points".
4. Practice and write long questions pointwise.
5. Practice map based questions.
6. Practice data based questions.
7. Practice previous years' question papers.
8. 3 hrs writing practice before the exam.
9. Revise your notes before the exam.
10. Mind map practice should be done.

During the exam

1) Read the question paper again and again, keep in mind what is being asked.
2) Solve the questions which you know well first.
3) Try to write neatly and cleanly.
4) Think about the questions which you are not able to understand and try to write the answer with discretion.
5) Keep in mind the word limit of the answers to the questions.
6) It is most important to take care of time management.
7) You can also write the answer with the help of picture or diagram or mind map.
8) There is no need to get distracted, solve the question paper with peace and patience.
9) Keep your balance, do not get overexcited and do not lose patience.
10) Don't forget to attach the map inside the answer sheet.

After the exam

1) Question paper and exam is just a medium to show how much you have learnt and presented it well. It does not mean that your learning ability has ended.
2) Wait for the exam result, accept whatever result comes and make a plan for future preparation and keep moving towards the goal with hard work and dedication.
3) Result is a new beginning, not the end.
4) Always be positive, your future is bright without any doubt.

God is with you with best wishes

Shailendra Singh, PGT (Geography), PM Shri School J.N.V. Gwalior (M.P.)